THAI

COOKING & MORE

Plus Japanese, Korean & Chinese

Publications International, Ltd.
Favorite Brand Name Recipes at www.fbnr.com

Pictured on the front cover: Beef and Asparagus Stir-Fry *(page 70).*
Pictured on the back cover *(top to bottom):* Thai Coconut Iced Tea *(page 20),* Rice Noodles with Broccoli and Tofu *(page 88)* and Spicy Thai Warm Shrimp Salad *(page 30).*

Illustrated by Joyce Shelton.

ISBN-13: 978-1-4127-9583-8
ISBN-10: 1-4127-9583-4

Library of Congress Control Number: 2008923760

Manufactured in China.

8 7 6 5 4 3 2 1

Microwave Cooking: Microwave ovens vary in wattage. Use the cooking times as guidelines and check for doneness before adding more time.

Preparation/Cooking Times: Preparation times are based on the approximate amount of time required to assemble the recipe before cooking, baking, chilling or serving. These times include preparation steps such as measuring, chopping and mixing. The fact that some preparations and cooking can be done simultaneously is taken into account. Preparation of optional ingredients and serving suggestions is not included.

Contents

Thai Cooking
for American Kitchens

It's not surprising that Thai cuisine is becoming an American favorite. Thai food is fresh-tasting, healthy and easy to love. The good news is that creating Thai favorites in an ordinary home kitchen is easy with the recipes in this book and an understanding of a few simple techniques.

Thanks to geography and climate, Thailand has a natural abundance of fruit, vegetables, produce and fish. The cuisine takes advantage of this bounty by using a variety of cooking methods that bring out the texture and flavor of these ingredients. In this book you'll find recipes for salads, curries, soups, stir-fries and grilled offerings. No special equipment is needed, just a deep skillet or wok, a broiler or grill, and the usual saucepans, knives and cutting boards. In fact, in Thailand many cooks turn out an amazing variety of delicious dishes over a simple charcoal fire.

Thai cooking is about freshness of ingredients and balance of flavors. Each dish must have the right combination of four primary tastes: sweet, sour, hot and salty. While there are certainly basic rules, most Thai recipes also suggest that you "season according to your heart's desire." It is not only acceptable, but desirable, to adjust the level of heat from chilies or the saltiness from fish sauce to taste. In fact, the only "authentic" approach is one that pleases your palate.

Do purchase the freshest vegetables and highest quality meat or seafood to make the most of your Thai dining experience. It's wiser to substitute something that's in season (green beans for broccoli, for instance) than to precisely follow a recipe. You'll find that most of the kitchen work involved comes in the preparation of ingredients. Make sure you read through an entire recipe first and do all the necessary chopping and slicing ahead of time since most cooking times are short.

If you lived in Thailand you could purchase freshly made curry pastes, coconut milk and rice noodles at the open-air marketplace. Fortunately, most American supermarkets now stock jarred curry paste, canned coconut milk and dried rice noodles. More exotic items can be purchased at Asian markets or even online. See the glossary for a list of ingredients and suggested substitutions.

pg. 42

pg. 8
pg. 64
pg. 132

RICE REIGNS SUPREME

It is impossible to overestimate the importance of rice to Thai cuisine. The most common expression for eat is "kin khâo" or "eat rice," and the phrase "Have you eaten rice yet?" is a favorite Thai greeting.

Thailand's most famous rice is long-grain jasmine. It is also called fragrant rice because of its delightful, flowery scent. Imported Thai jasmine rice is frequently available in the Asian section of supermarkets and there are even some American-grown versions. Of course, any long-grain rice can be substituted, but you owe it to yourself to at least try the real thing.

COOKING JASMINE RICE

Thai cooks rinse their rice before cooking. This isn't because it's unsanitary. It's to rinse off some of the powder that makes cooked rice stickier and starchier. To rinse rice, place it in a bowl or saucepan, cover it with cool water and swish the rice around with your hand until the water becomes cloudy. Pour off the water and repeat the procedure twice more.

There is an easy method for adding the correct amount of water to your raw rice. Place it in a saucepan and cover with ¾ inch of water. Most Asian cooks (except the many who have rice cookers!) measure by placing an index finger into the rice. The water should come up to the first knuckle.

Bring the rice and water to a boil. Stir once, then tightly cover the saucepan, turn the heat down to very low and cook for 20 minutes without lifting the cover. Turn off the heat and let the rice rest for at least 10 minutes before fluffing with a fork and serving.

Two secrets to perfect rice:

1. Use Very Low Heat. If you don't have a burner that holds a low simmer, invest in a device called a heat diffuser or "flame tamer." This round perforated metal disc can be purchased in cookware and hardware stores for a few dollars. It rests right on the burner, under the saucepan, to keep the heat even.

2. Don't Peek! Once the saucepan is covered, don't open it until the 20 minutes are up. Even a small loss of heat can make a difference. In fact, there is an ancient Indonesian story that echoes this. Once upon a time, every rice pot in the kingdom was filled each day from one single grain of rice. The rice goddess who caused this miracle had one rule: Never open the rice pot while that one grain turned into enough to feed the entire family. Of course, one day someone became too curious and peeked. The rice goddess herself was in the pot, and she was angry. She decreed that from that day forward, rice had to be grown, measured and cooked in quantity.

GLOSSARY

Asian eggplant: This long, slender variety may be solid purple or marbled purple and white. It is sweeter than the larger common variety and does not need to be peeled or salted.

bamboo shoots: Cut from an edible species of bamboo plant when it first pokes through the ground, bamboo shoots are available canned and sliced. Rinse thoroughly to remove any metallic taste.

basil: Several varieties of basil are used in Asian cooking, including Thai basil which has an anise-mint flavor and purple stems, and holy basil, which has a sharp, spicy-hot taste. Ordinary sweet basil is quite close in flavor to Thai basil and is a readily available substitute.

bean sprouts: The crisp, delicate sprouts of mung beans are extremely perishable. Purchase bean sprouts that have their buds attached and that smell and look fresh, not musty or slimy. Refrigerate sprouts and use within a few days.

cellophane noodles: These clear thin noodles, sold in tangled bunches, are also called bean threads or glass noodles. They are made from mung bean flour, and like rice noodles, must be soaked before using.

chili oil: This fiery oil is made by infusing vegetable oil with hot chili peppers.

chili paste or chili-garlic paste: A seasoning paste made of hot red chili peppers and garlic, chili paste is a frequent ingredient in Asian cooking, especially Chinese recipes.

chili peppers: Both fresh and dried chili peppers are used. The Thai bird's-eye pepper is a small red chili that packs more heat than any other pepper except the habanero. For American cooks, serrano chili peppers or jalapeño peppers are fine substitutes.

Dried red chili peppers are even hotter than fresh ones and can be slightly tamed by removing the seeds. In many recipes in this book, dried red pepper flakes are called for instead of whole chilies as they are easier to find.

Fresh or dried, care should be taken when handling chili peppers since they can sting and irritate the skin. Wear rubber gloves when handling peppers and do not touch your eyes. Be sure to wash your hands and all surfaces and utensils that have been in contact with the peppers after handling.

cilantro (coriander): The coriander plant produces both the bright green, fresh-tasting leaves (cilantro) and the seeds which are called coriander. Cilantro is sometimes called Chinese parsley and is used in virtually every Asian cuisine.

coconut milk: Unsweetened canned coconut milk is available in the ethnic sections of most supermarkets. Do not confuse it with cream of coconut which is a sweetened product used in drinks like piña coladas. Nor is coconut milk the liquid inside a fresh coconut (that's coconut water).

fish sauce: This condiment is used in Southeast Asian cooking as soy sauce is in Chinese cuisine. Don't be put off by its funky aroma which diminishes with cooking. Fish sauce helps balance and complete many dishes. It is possible to substitute soy sauce, but the results will be different.

ginger: Fresh ginger is a bumpy, beige-colored root used in most Asian cuisines. The root may be stored refrigerated for several weeks. For longer storage, wrap and freeze it. Ground dried ginger is from the same plant, but is not an acceptable substitute as the flavor is quite different.

green curry paste: Made from green chili peppers, this paste is even hotter than the red. Other ingredients are very similar to those in red curry paste.

lemongrass: The flowery perfume of lemongrass is one of the most delightful elements of Thai cooking. Minced finely, lemongrass is part of many curry pastes. The stalks are also cut into large pieces and used to flavor foods, then removed before serving, rather like a bay leaf. To use fresh lemongrass, cut off the moist portion at the root end. Throw away the dry, fibrous stalk and the outer leaves. The tender white portion may then be minced and used. Lemongrass freezes well. Grated lemon peel may be substituted, but with a substantial difference in flavor.

masaman curry paste: This complex curry paste includes cinnamon and nutmeg, along with the usual garlic, ginger and red chili peppers.

red curry paste: This usually includes fresh red chili peppers, lemongrass, shallots, garlic, ginger, coriander and cumin. Red curry paste is quite spicy, so start by using a small amount and adjust to taste.

rice noodles: These semi-translucent dried noodles come in many sizes and have many names, including rice stick noodles, rice-flour noodles and pho noodles. Widths range from string thin (usually called rice vermicelli) to 1 inch wide. All rice noodles must be soaked or boiled before using and all may be used interchangeably provided soaking and cooking times are adjusted.

rice papers: Look for packages containing stacks of thin translucent rounds, 6 to 8 inches in diameter, in Asian markets. Rice papers look incredibly fragile, but are actually fairly easy to handle. After soaking they become soft, flexible and a bit stretchy.

rice vinegar: Asian rice vinegar is milder than Western vinegars. The kind labeled "seasoned rice vinegar" is used for sushi rice. Look for plain rice vinegar for other recipes. Cider vinegar may be substituted, although the flavor will be different.

sesame oil: Asian sesame oil is made from the pressing of toasted sesame seeds, so it is dark in color. (Don't confuse it with the clear sesame oil sold in health food stores.) It should be used only as a flavoring agent, not as a cooking oil since it will easily burn.

shiitake mushrooms: The meaty flesh of the shiitake has a full-bodied, savory flavor. Shiitakes are available both dried and fresh. Remove the tough stems before using. Dried shiitakes must be soaked for 30 minutes to rehydrate them.

soy sauce: An extremely important seasoning in all Asian cuisines, soy sauce was developed more than 3,000 years ago. There are many brands and varieties, so choose one that suits your taste.

tofu (bean curd): This high-protein, low-cholesterol food made from soybeans is bland itself but has an amazing ability to absorb flavors. Tofu is available in blocks with different textures from soft (silken tofu) to extra firm. Once the package is opened, tofu must be refrigerated and used within a few days.

Wraps, Salads & Sides

Thai meals are flexible and usually offer small bites
of a variety of flavors. Tempt your tastebuds with Crisp Fish Cakes
or a traditional Thai Grilled Beef Salad. From refreshingly cool
to hot and tingling, Thai cuisine is always fresh and fun.

Thai Salad Rolls with Spicy Sweet & Sour Sauce

Spicy Sweet & Sour Sauce (recipe page 10)
3 ounces thin rice noodles (rice vermicelli)
4 ounces large raw shrimp, peeled and deveined
1 medium cucumber, peeled, seeded and cut into matchstick pieces
½ cup fresh cilantro leaves
½ cup fresh mint leaves
1 large bunch green leaf lettuce or Boston bibb lettuce

1. Prepare Spicy Sweet & Sour Sauce; set aside. Soak noodles in hot water 10 minutes to soften. Rinse under cold running water to cool; drain.

2. Meanwhile, bring water to a boil in medium saucepan. Add shrimp; return to a boil. Cook 3 minutes or until shrimp turn pink and opaque; drain. When cool, cut each shrimp lengthwise in half.

3. To assemble rolls, arrange shrimp, noodles, cucumber, cilantro and mint in center of lettuce leaves and roll up. Serve with Spicy Sweet & Sour Sauce.

Makes 6 servings

continued on page 10

Thai Salad Rolls with Spicy Sweet & Sour Sauce

Thai Salad Rolls with Spicy Sweet & Sour Sauce, continued

Spicy Sweet & Sour Sauce

1 green onion with top
1 tablespoon cornstarch
2 tablespoons rice vinegar
¾ cup water
¼ cup packed brown sugar
½ teaspoon red pepper flakes
2 tablespoons finely grated turnip

1. Finely chop white part of green onion; cut green portion into thin, 1-inch strips. Reserve green strips for garnish.

2. Combine cornstarch and vinegar in small bowl; mix well. Set aside.

3. Combine water, brown sugar, red pepper flakes and chopped green onion in small saucepan; bring to a boil. Stir in cornstarch mixture. Return to a boil; cook 1 minute or until sauce is clear and thickened. Cool. Sprinkle with turnip and reserved green onion strips just before serving.

Spicy Thai Satay Dip

⅓ cup peanut butter
⅓ cup *French's®* Honey Dijon Mustard
⅓ cup fat-free chicken broth
1 tablespoon chopped peeled fresh ginger
1 tablespoon honey
1 tablespoon *Frank's® RedHot®* Cayenne Pepper Sauce
1 tablespoon teriyaki sauce
1 tablespoon grated orange peel
2 cloves garlic, minced

Combine all ingredients in large bowl. Cover and refrigerate. Serve with vegetables, chips or grilled meats.

Makes 4 (¼-cup) servings

Prep Time: 10 minutes

Turkey Thai Rolls

**¾ pound JENNIE-O TURKEY STORE® Deli Premium Seasoned Brown Sugar
  Roasted Turkey Breast**
½ cup lettuce leaves, julienne cut or shredded lettuce
½ cup carrots, shredded
3 tablespoons basil, fresh, julienne cut
3 tablespoons mint, fresh, chopped
3 tablespoons cilantro, fresh, chopped
⅓ cup cucumber, peeled, seeded, julienne strips
⅓ cup peanuts, toasted, chopped
6 rice paper wrappers*

DIPPING SAUCE
⅔ cup vinegar
6 tablespoons sugar
1 teaspoon chili paste
2 stalks green onion, chopped

**Rice paper is a thin, edible wrapper used in Southeast Asian cooking. It is available in Asian
markets and some supermarkets. (See glossary.)*

Mix JENNIE-O TURKEY STORE® Deli Premium Seasoned Brown Sugar Roasted
Turkey Breast, lettuce, carrots, basil, mint, cilantro, cucumber and peanuts
together in small bowl. Dip one rice paper wrapper into warm water, soaking
until soft; pat very dry. Lay paper on flat surface. Place portion of mixture in
center of rice paper. Fold paper in half over filling, tuck in sides and roll up,
eggroll fashion. Place seam side down and repeat with remaining papers and
ingredients. Cut each roll in half. To make dipping sauce, bring vinegar and
sugar to boil in small saucepan over medium heat, boiling 2 minutes to reduce
mixture. Remove from heat and stir in chili paste and green onion. Serve
dipping sauce with rolls.

Makes 12 servings

Variations: Any variety of JENNIE-O TURKEY STORE® turkey breast can be
used in this recipe. Add sweet red pepper or fresh thyme to the mixture. Place
mixture in eggroll wrappers and deep-fry 3 to 4 minutes until golden brown.

Prep Time: 30 minutes

Shrimp, Mushroom and Omelet Soup

10 to 12 **dried shiitake mushrooms (about 1 ounce)**
  3 **eggs**
  1 **tablespoon chopped fresh chives or minced green onion tops**
  2 **teaspoons vegetable oil**
  3 **cans (about 14 ounces each) chicken broth**
  2 **tablespoons oyster sauce**
12 **ounces medium raw shrimp, peeled and deveined**
  3 **cups lightly packed fresh spinach leaves, washed and stemmed**
  1 **tablespoon lime juice**
    Red pepper flakes

1. Place mushrooms in bowl; cover with hot water. Let stand 30 minutes or until caps are soft. Meanwhile, beat eggs and chives in small bowl with wire whisk until blended.

2. Heat 10- to 12-inch nonstick skillet over medium-high heat. Add oil and swirl to coat surface. Pour egg mixture into pan. Reduce heat to medium; cover and cook, without stirring, 2 minutes or until set on bottom. Slide spatula under omelet; lift omelet and tilt pan to allow uncooked egg to flow under. Repeat at several places around omelet.

3. Slide omelet onto flat plate. Hold another plate over omelet and turn omelet over. Slide omelet back into pan to cook other side about 20 seconds. Slide back onto plate. When cool enough to handle, roll up omelet. Slice into ¼-inch-wide strips.

4. Drain mushrooms; squeeze out excess water. Remove and discard stems. Slice caps into thin strips. Combine mushrooms, chicken broth and oyster sauce in large saucepan. Cover and bring to a boil over high heat. Reduce heat to low; cook 5 minutes. Increase heat to medium-high; add shrimp and cook 2 minutes or until shrimp turn pink and opaque. Add omelet strips and spinach; remove from heat. Cover and let stand 2 minutes or until spinach wilts slightly. Stir in lime juice. Ladle soup into bowls. Sprinkle with red pepper flakes.

Makes 6 servings

Shrimp, Mushroom and Omelet Soup

Butternut Squash in Coconut Milk

⅓ **cup sweetened flaked coconut**

2 **teaspoons vegetable oil**

½ **small onion, finely chopped**

2 **cloves garlic, minced**

1 **cup canned unsweetened coconut milk**

¼ **cup packed brown sugar**

1 **tablespoon fish sauce**

⅛ **to ¼ teaspoon red pepper flakes**

1 **butternut squash (about 2 pounds), peeled and cut into large cubes**

1 **tablespoon chopped fresh cilantro**

   Cilantro sprig and purple kale for garnish

1. Preheat oven to 350°F. Spread coconut in baking pan. Bake 6 minutes or until golden, stirring occasionally. Set aside to cool and crisp.

2. Heat oil in large saucepan over medium-high heat. Add onion and garlic; cook and stir 3 minutes or until tender. Add coconut milk, brown sugar, fish sauce and red pepper flakes; stir until sugar is dissolved.

3. Bring mixture to a boil; add squash. Reduce heat to medium; cover and simmer 30 minutes or until squash is tender. Transfer squash to serving bowl with slotted spoon.

4. Increase heat to high; boil remaining liquid until thick, stirring constantly. Pour liquid over squash in bowl. Sprinkle with toasted coconut and chopped cilantro. Garnish, if desired.

Makes 4 to 6 servings

Butternut Squash in Coconut Milk

Crisp Fish Cakes

Ginger Dipping Sauce (recipe page 18)
1 **pound boneless catfish, halibut or cod fillets, cut into 1-inch pieces**
1 **tablespoon fish sauce**
3 **cloves garlic, minced**
1 **tablespoon chopped fresh cilantro**
2 **teaspoons grated lemon peel**
1 **teaspoon finely chopped fresh ginger**
$\frac{1}{8}$ **teaspoon ground red pepper**
 Peanut oil for frying
1 **head curly leaf lettuce**
1 **medium green or red apple, cut into thin strips *or* 1 ripe mango, diced**
$\frac{1}{2}$ **cup fresh cilantro leaves**
$\frac{1}{3}$ **cup fresh mint leaves**

1. Prepare Ginger Dipping Sauce; set aside. Process fish pieces in food processor just until coarsely chopped. Add fish sauce, garlic, chopped cilantro, lemon peel, ginger and red pepper; process until combined. Place fish mixture on oiled cutting board; pat evenly into 7-inch square. Cut into 16 squares; shape each square into 2-inch patty.

2. Heat 1 to 1½ inches oil in Dutch oven or large skillet over medium-high heat to 360°F to 375°F. Fry patties in batches 2 to 3 minutes or until golden and fish is opaque in center. (Do not crowd pan; allow oil to return to temperature between batches.)

3. Serve with lettuce leaves, apple, cilantro leaves, mint and Ginger Dipping Sauce. To eat, stack 1 fish cake, apple strips, cilantro and mint in center of lettuce leaf. Drizzle with sauce; enclose filling in lettuce leaf.

Makes 6 to 8 servings

continued on page 18

Crisp Fish Cakes

Crisp Fish Cakes, continued

Ginger Dipping Sauce

¼ **cup rice vinegar**
2 **tablespoons water**
1 **teaspoon sugar**
1 **teaspoon finely chopped fresh ginger**
½ **teaspoon red pepper flakes**
½ **teaspoon fish sauce**

Combine all ingredients in small bowl; stir until sugar dissolves.

Makes about ⅓ cup

Thai Summer Rolls

Dipping Sauce (recipe follows)
8 **ounces medium raw shrimp, peeled and deveined**
3½ **ounces thin rice noodles (rice vermicelli)**
12 **rice paper wrappers* (6½ inches in diameter)**
36 **whole fresh cilantro leaves**
4 **ounces roast pork or beef, sliced ⅛ inch thick**
1 **tablespoon chopped peanuts**
Lime peel for garnish

*Rice paper is a thin, edible wrapper used in Southeast Asian cooking. It is available in Asian markets and some supermarkets. (See glossary.)

1. Prepare Dipping Sauce; set aside. Bring large saucepan of water to a boil. Add shrimp; simmer 1 to 2 minutes or until pink and opaque. Remove shrimp, cool and slice in half lengthwise.

2. Meanwhile, add rice vermicelli to saucepan. Cook until tender but still firm, about 3 minutes. Drain and rinse under cold running water.

3. Soften rice paper wrappers in large bowl of warm water 30 to 40 seconds. Drain wrappers on paper towels. Place one at a time on cutting board. Arrange cilantro leaves in center of wrapper. Layer with 2 shrimp halves, pork and rice vermicelli. Fold bottom of wrapper over filling; fold in each side and roll up, burrito-style. Repeat with remaining wrappers.

4. Sprinkle summer rolls with peanuts. Serve with Dipping Sauce.

Makes 12 summer rolls

Dipping Sauce

½ **cup water**
¼ **cup fish sauce**
2 **tablespoons lime juice**
1 **tablespoon sugar**
1 **clove garlic, minced**
¼ **teaspoon chili oil**

Combine all ingredients in small bowl; mix well.

Makes about 1 cup

tip

Rice papers look incredibly fragile, but are actually fairly easy to work with, once you get the knack. After soaking they become soft, flexible and a bit stretchy. You can allow everyone at the dinner table to assemble their own summer rolls instead of doing it ahead of time if you like. Just set out the assorted fillings and provide softened rice papers for a do-it-yourself Thai appetizer.

Thai Coconut Iced Tea

2 jasmine tea bags
2 cups boiling water
1 cup coconut milk
2 tablespoons sugar *or* 2 packets no-calorie sweetener

1. Brew 2 cups jasmine tea with boiling water according to package instructions; cool to room temperature.

2. Pour ½ cup coconut milk into each glass. Stir 1 tablespoon sugar into each glass. Add ice, then carefully pour ½ of tea into each glass and serve immediately.

Makes 2 servings

Tip: For a more dramatic presentation, gently pour tea over the back of a spoon held close to the surface of the coconut milk in each glass. The tea will pool in a layer on the coconut milk before combining.

Jasmine tea is made by layering green tea leaves with jasmine flowers so that their delicate scent permeates the tea. Some loose leaf jasmine teas still have flowers in the mix which the hot water causes to "bloom" when you brew the tea. If you enjoy the flavor and aroma of jasmine tea, you can also use the tea to flavor rice, sauces or even ice cream.

Thai Coconut Iced Tea

Thai Chicken Broccoli Salad

4 ounces uncooked linguine
   Nonstick cooking spray
½ pound boneless skinless chicken breasts, cut into 2×½-inch pieces
2 cups broccoli florets
2 tablespoons cold water
⅔ cup chopped red bell pepper
6 green onions, sliced diagonally into 1-inch pieces
¼ cup creamy peanut butter
2 tablespoons hot water
2 tablespoons soy sauce
2 teaspoons dark sesame oil
½ teaspoon red pepper flakes
⅛ teaspoon garlic powder
¼ cup unsalted peanuts, chopped

1. Cook pasta according to package directions. Drain; set aside.

2. Spray large nonstick skillet with cooking spray; heat over medium-high heat. Add chicken; stir-fry 5 minutes or until chicken is no longer pink. Remove chicken from skillet.

3. Add broccoli and cold water to skillet. Cook, covered, 2 minutes. Uncover; cook and stir 2 minutes or until broccoli is crisp-tender. Remove broccoli from skillet. Combine pasta, chicken, broccoli, bell pepper and onions in large bowl.

4. Blend peanut butter, hot water, soy sauce, oil, red pepper flakes and garlic powder in small bowl. Drizzle over pasta mixture; toss to coat. Top with peanuts before serving.

Makes 4 servings

Thai Chicken Broccoli Salad

Thai Noodle Soup

1 package (3 ounces) ramen noodles
¾ pound chicken tenders
2 cans (about 14 ounces each) chicken broth
¼ cup shredded carrot
¼ cup frozen snow peas
2 tablespoons thinly sliced green onions
½ teaspoon minced garlic
¼ teaspoon ground ginger
3 tablespoons chopped fresh cilantro
½ lime, cut into 4 wedges

1. Break noodles into pieces. Cook noodles according to package directions (discard flavor packet). Drain and set aside.

2. Cut chicken tenders into ½-inch pieces. Combine chicken broth and chicken tenders in large saucepan or Dutch oven; bring to a boil over medium heat. Cook 2 minutes.

3. Add carrot, snow peas, green onions, garlic and ginger. Reduce heat to low; simmer 3 minutes. Add cooked noodles and cilantro; heat through. Serve soup with lime wedges.

Makes 4 servings

Prep and Cook Time: 15 minutes

Thai Noodle Soup

Thai Grilled Beef Salad

3 tablespoons Thai seasoning,* divided

1 beef flank steak (about 1 pound)

2 tablespoons chopped fresh cilantro

2 tablespoons chopped fresh basil

2 red Thai chili peppers *or* 1 red jalapeño pepper,** seeded and sliced into thin slivers

1 tablespoon finely chopped lemongrass

1 tablespoon minced red onion

1 clove garlic, minced

Juice of 1 lime

1 tablespoon fish sauce

1 large carrot, grated

1 cucumber, chopped

4 cups assorted salad greens

*Thai seasoning usually includes chili peppers, garlic, ginger, coriander, lime and basil.

**Thai chili peppers and jalapeño peppers can sting and irritate the skin; wear rubber gloves when handling peppers and do not touch eyes. Wash hands after handling.

1. Prepare grill for direct grilling.

2. Sprinkle 1 tablespoon Thai seasoning over beef; turn to coat. Cover and marinate 15 minutes. Place beef on grid over medium heat. Grill, uncovered, 17 to 21 minutes for medium rare to medium or until desired doneness, turning once. Cool 10 minutes.

3. Meanwhile, combine remaining 2 tablespoons Thai seasoning, cilantro, basil, chili peppers, lemongrass, onion, garlic, lime juice and fish sauce in medium bowl; mix well.

4. Thinly slice beef across grain. Add beef, carrot and cucumber to dressing; toss to coat. Arrange on bed of greens.

Makes 4 servings

Thai Grilled Beef Salad

Thai Lamb & Couscous Rolls

5 cups water, divided

16 large napa or Chinese cabbage leaves, stems trimmed

2 tablespoons minced fresh ginger

1 teaspoon red pepper flakes

⅔ cup couscous

   Nonstick cooking spray

½ pound lean ground lamb

½ cup chopped green onions

3 cloves garlic, minced

¼ cup plus 2 tablespoons minced fresh cilantro or mint, divided

2 tablespoons soy sauce

1 tablespoon lime juice

1 teaspoon dark sesame oil

1 cup plain yogurt

1. Place 4 cups water in medium saucepan; bring to a boil over high heat. Drop cabbage leaves into water; cook 30 seconds. Drain. Rinse under cold water until cool; pat dry with paper towels.

2. Place 1 cup water, ginger and red pepper flakes in medium saucepan; bring to a boil over high heat. Stir in couscous; cover. Remove saucepan from heat; let stand 5 minutes.

3. Spray large skillet with cooking spray; add lamb, green onions and garlic. Cook and stir over medium-high heat 5 minutes or until lamb is no longer pink; drain.

4. Combine couscous, lamb mixture, ¼ cup cilantro, soy sauce, lime juice and sesame oil in medium bowl. Spoon mixture evenly down center of cabbage leaves. Fold ends of cabbage leaves over filling; roll up. Combine yogurt and remaining 2 tablespoons cilantro in small bowl; spoon evenly over rolls. Serve warm. Garnish, if desired.

Makes 16 servings

Thai Lamb & Couscous Rolls

Spicy Thai Warm Shrimp Salad

¾ **cup prepared vinaigrette salad dressing**

⅓ **cup chopped fresh mint leaves**

¼ **cup** *Frank's® RedHot®* **XTRA Hot Sauce or** *Frank's® RedHot®* **Cayenne Pepper Sauce**

¼ **cup** *French's®* **Honey Dijon Mustard**

1 **tablespoon lime juice**

1 **tablespoon sucralose sugar substitute**

1 **tablespoon vegetable oil**

1½ **pounds large shrimp, shelled with tails left on**

8 **cups shredded Napa cabbage**

1 **red bell pepper, thinly sliced**

1 **cup thinly sliced cucumber**

1. Combine salad dressing, mint, XTRA Hot Sauce, mustard, lime juice and sugar substitute in large bowl; set aside.

2. Heat oil in large nonstick skillet or wok until hot. Stir-fry shrimp 2 to 3 minutes until shrimp turn pink. Transfer to bowl with dressing. Add cabbage, bell pepper and cucumber; toss to coat. Serve warm.

Makes 6 servings

Prep Time: 10 minutes
Cook Time: 5 minutes

Spicy Thai Warm Shrimp Salad

Thai Turkey Soup

6 ounces uncooked linguine
½ cup roasted unsalted peanuts
 Grated peel and juice of 1 lemon
1 piece (1½×1 inch) fresh ginger, peeled and quartered
3 large cloves garlic
1 tablespoon sugar
1 teaspoon ground cumin
¼ to ½ teaspoon cayenne pepper
1 medium red onion, quartered
1 tablespoon vegetable oil
3 cups homemade turkey broth *or* 2 cans (14 ounces each) chicken broth
1 can (14 ounces) coconut milk
2 cups cubed grilled turkey
2 tablespoons lime juice
 Salt and black pepper
 Sliced green onions
 Chopped cilantro
 Lime wedges

1. Cook linguine according to package directions; drain and set aside. Place peanuts in food processor; process with on/off pulsing action until chopped. Do not overprocess. Remove 2 tablespoons chopped peanuts; reserve for garnish. Add peel, lemon juice, ginger, garlic, sugar, cumin, cayenne pepper and 1 red onion quarter to remaining peanuts in food processor. Process about 1 minute until mixture forms smooth paste, scraping sides of food processor container as needed.

2. Heat oil in 5-quart Dutch oven over medium heat; add peanut mixture. Cook 5 minutes, stirring frequently. Meanwhile, slice remaining 3 red onion quarters into thin slivers. Add broth, coconut milk and onion slivers to Dutch oven; bring to a boil over high heat. Reduce heat to medium; cook 8 minutes, stirring occasionally. Add linguine, turkey and lime juice; heat through. Season to taste with salt and black pepper. Garnish each serving with green onions, cilantro and lime wedges. Sprinkle with reserved chopped peanuts.

Makes 6 servings

Hot to Go Thai Salad

¾ **pound beef sirloin steak**

⅓ **cup vegetable oil, divided**

⅓ **cup rice vinegar***

¼ **cup reduced-sodium soy sauce**

1 **fresh jalapeño or serrano pepper, finely chopped, divided**

2 **cloves garlic, minced**

1 **tablespoon minced fresh gingerroot**

½ **teaspoon red pepper flakes**

1 **(9-ounce) package French-style green beans, thawed and drained**

2 **carrots, halved and thinly sliced**

1 **cucumber, peeled, seeded and sliced**

4 **cups cooked brown rice**

Chopped fresh mint leaves (optional)

White wine vinegar can be substituted.

Partially freeze steak; slice across grain into ¼-inch strips. Place in large bowl. Combine all but 1 tablespoon oil, vinegar, soy sauce, ½ of the jalapeño, garlic, gingerroot and red pepper flakes in small bowl. Pour mixture over beef; marinate 1 hour. Drain beef; discard marinade. Heat remaining 1 tablespoon vegetable oil in large skillet over medium-high heat until hot. Add beef and remaining jalapeño; cook 3 to 5 minutes or until no longer pink. Combine beef, liquid from skillet, beans, carrots, cucumber and rice in large bowl. Toss to coat. Sprinkle with mint, if desired.

Makes 6 servings

Favorite recipe from **USA Rice**

Thai-Style Salad with Shredded Glazed Chicken

1 head Napa cabbage or romaine lettuce, shredded (about 6 cups)

1 medium cucumber, peeled, halved lengthwise, seeded and sliced (about 1¼ cups)

2 medium carrots, coarsely grated (about 1 cup)

2 small oranges, peeled and cut into segments

½ cup fresh cilantro leaves (optional)

2 Honey-Lime Glazed Chicken Breasts, shredded (recipe page 52)

Honey-Lime Dressing (recipe follows)

¼ cup dry-roasted peanuts, chopped

Combine all ingredients except Honey-Lime Dressing and peanuts in large bowl; toss until well blended. Pour Honey-Lime Dressing over salad; toss until well blended. Sprinkle each serving with peanuts just before serving.

Makes 4 servings

Honey-Lime Dressing: Whisk together 6 tablespoons honey, 3 tablespoons peanut butter, 3 tablespoons lime juice, 2 tablespoons chopped fresh mint, 1 tablespoon minced seeded jalapeño pepper, 1½ teaspoons soy sauce, 1 teaspoon minced garlic and ¾ teaspoon grated lime peel in small bowl until well blended.

Favorite recipe from **National Honey Board**

Thai-Style Salad with Shredded Glazed Chicken

Thai-Style Tuna and Fruit Salad with Sweet-Sour-Spicy Dressing

8 lettuce leaves (use different varieties for color)
2 tablespoons chopped fresh cilantro
2 tablespoons chopped fresh mint leaves
1 (3-ounce) pouch of STARKIST Flavor Fresh Pouch® Albacore Tuna
⅓ cup sliced cucumber
⅓ cup drained mandarin oranges
⅓ cup red seedless grape halves
¼ cup thinly sliced red onion
Sweet-Sour-Spicy Dressing (recipe follows)
⅓ cup chopped cashews or peanuts

On platter, arrange half of lettuce. Break up remaining lettuce into bite-size pieces and place on lettuce on platter. Sprinkle cilantro and mint over lettuce. Arrange tuna, cucumber, oranges, grapes and onion on top. Refrigerate, covered, while preparing Sweet-Sour-Spicy Dressing. Pour dressing over salad; sprinkle with cashews.

Makes 4 servings

Variation: Chop or tear all lettuce into bite-sized pieces; combine with remaining ingredients. Toss with dressing.

Sweet-Sour-Spicy Dressing

Lime
3 cloves garlic
2 serrano chilies, halved, seeded and cut in pieces
¼ cup lime juice
1½ tablespoons nam pla (fish sauce) or soy sauce
1 tablespoon sugar

Peel ½ of lime with vegetable peeler. Place peel in blender or small food processor; add garlic, chilies, lime juice, nam pla and sugar. Process until mixture is blended and lime peel, garlic and chilies are finely chopped.

Prep Time: 20 minutes

Thai-Style Tuna and Fruit Salad
with Sweet-Sour-Spicy Dressing

Thai Peanut Salad

1 cup picante sauce
¼ cup chunky-style peanut butter
2 tablespoons honey
2 tablespoons orange juice
1 teaspoon soy sauce
½ teaspoon ground ginger
2 cups (12 ounces) chopped CURE 81® ham
1 (7-ounce) package spaghetti, cooked
¼ cup dry roasted unsalted peanuts
¼ cup red bell pepper, cut into julienne strips
2 tablespoons chopped cilantro

In small saucepan, combine picante sauce, peanut butter, honey, orange juice, soy sauce and ginger. Cook, stirring over low heat until mixture is smooth. Add ¼ cup sauce mixture to ham. Gently toss remaining sauce mixture with hot cooked pasta. Toss pasta mixture with ham mixture, peanuts and pepper strips. Cover and chill 1 to 2 hours. Before serving, sprinkle with cilantro.

Makes 4 servings

tip

When purchasing cilantro look for bright green leaves with no signs of yellowing or wilting. To keep cilantro fresh longer, place the stem ends in a glass of water (like a bouquet), cover loosely with a plastic bag and refrigerate. Wait to wash and chop the herbs until just before using.

Thai Peanut Salad

From the Land

Thai cooking is famous for great grilled dishes, and it's easy to create the smoky savor of a satay or Thai Grilled Chicken at home. Thai curries are legendary with good reason, too. The layering of flavors adds depth to chicken, beef or pork.

Thai Barbecued Chicken

1 cup coarsely chopped fresh cilantro
2 jalapeño peppers, coarsely chopped
8 cloves garlic, peeled and coarsely chopped
2 tablespoons fish sauce
1 tablespoon packed brown sugar
1 teaspoon curry powder
   Grated peel of 1 lemon
3 pounds chicken pieces

1. Place cilantro, jalapeño peppers, garlic, fish sauce, brown sugar, curry powder and lemon peel in blender or food processor; blend to form coarse paste.

2. Work fingers between skin and meat on breast and thigh pieces. Rub seasoning paste under skin and on all sides of each chicken piece. Place chicken in large resealable food storage bag or covered container; marinate in refrigerator 3 to 4 hours or overnight.

3. Prepare grill for direct cooking. Grill chicken over medium coals, skin side down, 10 minutes. Turn chicken and grill 20 to 30 minutes more or until cooked through (170°F for breast meat, 180°F for dark meat). Thighs and legs may require 10 to 15 minutes more cooking time than breasts.

Makes 4 servings

Thai Barbecued Chicken

Thai Duck with Beans and Sprouts

2 tablespoons soy sauce
2 tablespoons vegetable oil, divided
   Juice of 1 lime
1 tablespoon fish sauce
2 teaspoons minced fresh ginger
2 cloves garlic, minced
1 pound boneless skinless duck breast, cut into ½-inch strips
3 cups fresh green beans
1 cup chicken broth
4 green onions, sliced
1½ cups bean sprouts

1. Combine soy sauce, 1 tablespoon oil, lime juice, fish sauce, ginger and garlic in medium bowl. Add duck; stir to coat well. Cover and refrigerate 45 minutes to 8 hours.

2. Heat remaining 1 tablespoon oil in large skillet or wok over high heat. Remove duck from marinade, reserve marinade. Add duck to skillet and stir-fry 4 to 6 minutes or until no longer pink. Remove duck with slotted spoon.

3. Add green beans to skillet; stir-fry 5 to 6 minutes or until green beans are crisp-tender. Add chicken broth, green onions and reserved marinade to skillet; boil 2 minutes. Return duck and accumulated juices to skillet and add bean sprouts. Cook and stir until heated through.

Makes 4 servings

tip

Stir-fries depend on high heat and fast cooking. Small pieces of food, such as the duck in this recipe, can overcook in a matter of seconds, so it is important to remove them from the skillet or wok as directed. Keep a large shallow dish or plate beside the stove to hold the cooked ingredients and any accumulated juice until it's time to return everything to the skillet near the end of the cooking time.

Thai Duck with Beans and Sprouts

Exotic Pork & Vegetables

¼ cup water

2 teaspoons cornstarch

4 tablespoons peanut oil, divided

6 whole dried hot red chili peppers

4 cloves garlic, sliced

1 pork tenderloin (about ¾ pound), thinly sliced

1 large carrot, peeled*

2 ounces fresh oyster, shiitake or button mushrooms,** cut into halves

1 baby eggplant, thinly sliced

1 package (about 5 ounces) fresh snow peas, ends trimmed

3 tablespoons packed brown sugar

2 tablespoons fish sauce

1 tablespoon dark sesame oil

   Hot cooked rice

To make scalloped edges on carrot, use citrus stripper or grapefruit spoon to cut groove into carrot, cutting lengthwise from stem end to tip. Continue to cut grooves around carrot about ¼ inch apart. Cut carrot crosswise into ¼-inch-thick slices.

**Or, substitute ½ ounce dried Oriental mushrooms, soaked according to package directions.*

1. Combine water and cornstarch in cup; set aside.

2. Heat large skillet or wok over high heat 1 minute. Drizzle 2 tablespoons peanut oil into skillet and heat 30 seconds. Add peppers and garlic; stir-fry about 1 minute. Add pork; stir-fry 3 to 4 minutes or until no longer pink. Remove pork mixture to bowl and set aside.

3. Add remaining 2 tablespoons peanut oil to skillet. Add carrot, mushrooms and eggplant; stir-fry 2 minutes. Add snow peas and pork mixture; stir-fry 1 minute.

4. Stir cornstarch mixture; add to skillet. Cook 1 minute or until thickened. Stir in brown sugar, fish sauce and sesame oil; cook until heated through. Serve over rice.

Makes 4 servings

Exotic Pork & Vegetables

Thai Chicken with Basil

1 small bunch fresh basil, divided

2 cups vegetable oil

6 large shallots, coarsely chopped

5 cloves garlic, minced

1 piece fresh ginger (about 1 inch square), peeled and cut into thin strips

1 pound ground chicken or turkey

2 fresh Thai chili peppers or jalapeño peppers,* cut into thin slices

2 teaspoons brown sugar

1/2 teaspoon salt

Boston lettuce leaves

Japanese mizuna, cherry tomatoes and additional Thai peppers for garnish

Thai chili peppers and jalapeño peppers can sting and irritate the skin; wear rubber gloves when handling chilies and do not touch eyes. Wash hands after handling.

1. Set aside 8 small basil sprigs. Slice remaining basil into strips; set aside.

2. Heat oil in wok over medium-high heat until oil registers 375°F on deep-fry thermometer. Add 1 or 2 basil sprigs and deep-fry about 15 seconds or until basil is glossy and crisp. Remove fried sprig with slotted spoon to paper towels; drain. Repeat with remaining sprigs, reheating oil between batches. Reserve fried basil.

3. Let oil cool slightly. Pour off oil; measure 1/4 cup oil and return to wok. Heat over medium-high heat 30 seconds. (Reserve remaining oil for another use.) Add shallots, garlic and ginger; cook and stir 1 minute. Add chicken and stir-fry about 4 minutes or until lightly browned. Push chicken up side of wok, letting juices remain in bottom.

4. Continue to cook about 5 to 7 minutes or until all liquid evaporates. Stir in chili pepper slices, brown sugar and salt; cook 1 minute. Stir in reserved basil strips. Remove from heat.

5. Line serving plate with lettuce. Spoon chicken mixture on top. Top with reserved fried basil. Garnish, if desired.

Makes 4 servings

Thai Chicken with Basil

Caramelized Lemongrass Chicken

1½ **pounds skinless chicken thighs (4 to 6 thighs)**
  2 **stalks lemongrass**
  3 **tablespoons fish sauce**
  ¼ **cup sugar**
  2 **cloves garlic, slivered**
  ¼ **teaspoon black pepper**
  1 **tablespoon vegetable oil**
  1 **tablespoon lemon juice**

1. Rinse chicken and pat dry with paper towels.

2. Remove outer leaves from lemongrass and discard. Trim off and discard upper stalks. Flatten lemongrass with meat mallet. Cut lemongrass into 1-inch pieces.

3. Place chicken in large resealable plastic food storage bag; add fish sauce, sugar, garlic, pepper and lemongrass. Seal bag tightly; turn to coat. Marinate in refrigerator at least 1 hour or up to 4 hours, turning occasionally.

4. Heat oil in large skillet over medium heat. Remove chicken from food storage bag; reserve marinade. Cook chicken 10 minutes or until browned, turning once.

5. Pour reserved marinade into skillet; bring to a boil. Boil 1 to 2 minutes. Reduce heat to low; cover and simmer 30 minutes or until chicken is tender and no longer pink in center, turning chicken occasionally.

6. Stir lemon juice into skillet. Turn chicken pieces over to coat. Garnish as desired.

Makes 4 servings

Caramelized Lemongrass Chicken

Sesame Pork with Thai Cucumber Salad

1 large or 2 small pork tenderloins (about 1¼ pounds total)
¼ cup soy sauce
2 cloves garlic, minced
   Thai Cucumber Salad (recipe page 52)
3 tablespoons honey
2 tablespoons brown sugar
1 teaspoon minced fresh ginger
1 to 2 tablespoons toasted sesame seeds*

*To toast sesame seeds, spread seeds in small skillet. Shake skillet over medium heat 2 minutes or until seeds begin to pop and turn golden.

1. Place pork in large resealable food storage bag. Combine soy sauce and garlic in small cup; pour over pork. Close bag securely; turn to coat. Marinate in refrigerator up to 2 hours. Meanwhile prepare Thai Cucumber Salad and refrigerate.

2. Preheat oven to 400°F. Drain pork; reserve 1 tablespoon marinade. Combine honey, brown sugar, ginger and reserved marinade in small bowl.

3. Place pork in shallow foil-lined roasting pan. Brush with half of honey mixture. Roast 10 minutes. Turn pork over; brush with remaining honey mixture; sprinkle with sesame seeds. Roast 10 minutes for small or 15 minutes for large tenderloin or until internal temperature reaches 155°F when tested with meat thermometer inserted into thickest part of pork.

4. Let pork stand, tented with foil, on cutting board 5 minutes. (Temperature of pork will rise to 160°F.) Cut into ½-inch slices and serve with Thai Cucumber Salad.

Makes 4 servings

continued on page 52

Sesame Pork with Thai Cucumber Salad

Sesame Pork with Thai Cucumber Salad, continued

Thai Cucumber Salad

1 large European-style cucumber
¼ medium red onion, thinly sliced
¼ cup rice wine vinegar
2 tablespoons lime juice
1 heaping teaspoon sugar
2 tablespoons chopped fresh cilantro
2 tablespoons chopped unsalted peanuts

Wash, but do not peel, cucumber; cut into thin slices. Mix cucumber and onion in medium bowl. Combine vinegar, lime juice and sugar in small bowl; stir into cucumber mixture. Cover and refrigerate salad at least 30 minutes. Stir in cilantro and top with peanuts before serving.

Honey-Lime Glazed Chicken

½ cup honey
2 tablespoons lime juice
2 tablespoons chopped fresh cilantro
1 tablespoon soy sauce
2 teaspoons seeded, minced jalapeño pepper
1½ teaspoon minced garlic
6 bone-in chicken breast halves (about 3 pounds)

Blend all ingredients except chicken in small bowl. Place chicken in shallow baking dish; pour half of marinade over chicken. Cover and refrigerate 2 hours or overnight. Reserve remaining marinade. Grill chicken over medium-hot coals about 15 minutes, turning and basting with reserved marinade, or until chicken is no longer pink in center. If desired, reserve 2 chicken breasts for use in Thai-Style Salad with Shredded Glazed Chicken (recipe page 34).

Makes 6 servings

*Favorite recipe from **National Honey Board***

Thai Loin Steaks with Black Bean Relish

1 stalk lemongrass, outer leaves and tough upper stalk removed

1 tablespoon sugar

1 tablespoon fish sauce

1 teaspoon minced garlic

1/2 to 1 teaspoon hot chili oil

2 boneless beef top loin (strip) steaks (8 ounces each)

1 can (about 8¾ ounces) whole baby corn (about 8 cobs), rinsed and drained

1 can (about 15 ounces) black beans, rinsed and drained

1 cup diced mango

1/2 green bell pepper, cut into strips

2 tablespoons chopped red onion

1 jalapeño pepper,* seeded and sliced (optional)

Juice of 1/2 lemon

1/2 teaspoon vegetable oil

1/2 teaspoon honey

1/8 teaspoon salt

Jalapeños can sting and irritate the skin; wear rubber gloves when handling and do not touch eyes. Wash hands after handling.

1. Flatten lemongrass with meat mallet and mince. Combine with sugar, fish sauce, garlic and chili oil in baking dish. Cut each steak lengthwise into 2 strips. Place in dish with marinade, coating both sides. Cover; refrigerate 1 hour, turning once.

2. Halve corn cobs diagonally; combine with beans, mango, bell pepper, onion and jalapeño, if desired, in large bowl. Combine lemon juice, oil, honey and salt in small bowl; stir into bean mixture.

3. Grill steaks over medium heat, uncovered, 10 to 12 minutes for medium-rare to medium or until desired doneness, turning once. Serve with relish.

Makes 4 servings

Pineapple Basil Chicken Supreme

1 can (8 ounces) pineapple chunks in unsweetened juice

2 teaspoons cornstarch

2 tablespoons peanut oil

3 boneless skinless chicken breasts (about 1 pound), cut into ¾-inch pieces

2 to 4 serrano peppers,* cut into thin strips

2 cloves garlic, minced

2 green onions, cut into 1-inch pieces

¾ cup roasted, unsalted cashews

¼ cup chopped fresh basil (do not use dried)

1 tablespoon fish sauce

1 tablespoon soy sauce

　Hot cooked rice

Serrano peppers can sting and irritate the skin; wear rubber gloves when handling peppers and do not touch eyes. Wash hands after handling.

1. Drain pineapple, reserving juice. Combine reserved juice and cornstarch in small bowl; set aside.

2. Heat wok over high heat 1 minute. Drizzle oil into wok and heat 30 seconds. Add chicken, peppers and garlic; stir-fry 3 minutes or until chicken is no longer pink. Add green onions; stir-fry 1 minute. Stir cornstarch mixture; add to wok. Cook 1 minute or until thickened. Add pineapple, cashews, basil, fish sauce and soy sauce; stir-fry 1 minute or until heated through. Serve over rice.

Makes 4 servings

Pineapple Basil Chicken Supreme

Masaman Curry Beef

Masaman Curry Paste (recipe page 58) *or* jarred Masaman curry paste
   to taste

4 tablespoons vegetable oil, divided

1 medium onion, cut into strips

1½ pounds boneless beef chuck, cut into 1-inch cubes

2 cans (about 14 ounces each) unsweetened coconut milk

3 tablespoons fish sauce

2 pounds boiling potatoes, peeled and cut into 1½-inch pieces

1 large red bell pepper, cut into strips

½ cup roasted peanuts, chopped

2 tablespoons lime juice

¼ cup slivered fresh basil leaves or chopped fresh cilantro

   Hot cooked rice or noodles

1. Prepare Masaman Curry Paste; set aside.

2. Heat 1 tablespoon oil in large skillet or wok over medium-high heat. Add onion; stir-fry 6 minutes or until golden. Transfer to bowl with slotted spoon.

3. Add 1 tablespoon oil to skillet. Increase heat to high. Add half the beef; stir-fry 2 to 3 minutes until browned on all sides. Transfer beef to another bowl; set aside. Repeat with remaining beef, adding 1 tablespoon oil to prevent sticking if necessary.

4. Reduce heat to medium. Add remaining 1 tablespoon oil and curry paste to skillet; cook and stir 1 to 2 minutes. Add coconut milk and fish sauce; stir to scrape bits of cooked meat and spices from bottom of wok. Return beef to wok; bring to a boil. Reduce heat; cover and simmer 45 minutes.

5. Add potatoes and onion to wok. Cook 35 to 45 minutes more or until meat and potatoes are fork-tender. Stir in bell pepper; cook until heated through.

6. Stir in peanuts and lime juice; sprinkle with basil. Serve with rice or noodles.

Makes 8 servings

continued on page 58

Masaman Curry Beef

Masaman Curry Beef, continued

Masaman Curry Paste

6 tablespoons coarsely chopped fresh ginger
3 tablespoons coarsely chopped garlic (10 to 12 cloves)
2 tablespoons ground cumin
1 tablespoon ground mace or nutmeg
1 tablespoon packed brown sugar
2 teaspoons grated lemon peel
2 teaspoons ground cinnamon
2 to 4 teaspoons ground red pepper*
2 teaspoons paprika
2 teaspoons black pepper
2 teaspoons anchovy paste *or* 1 minced anchovy fillet
1 teaspoon turmeric
1 teaspoon ground cloves

*Use 2 teaspoons ground red pepper for mild paste and up to 4 teaspoons for very hot paste.

Place all ingredients in food processor or blender; process until paste forms.

Makes about ½ cup

tip

Curry pastes are the heart and soul of Thai cooking.
Making your own curry paste, as in the above recipe, is not difficult.
While it is fairly easy to find prepared curry pastes in larger supermarkets,
blending your own allows you to tailor the flavor to your taste.
Feel free to adjust amounts of ingredients to suit your palate.

Thai Pumpkin Satay

1 cup LIBBY'S® 100% Pure Pumpkin

⅔ cup milk

⅓ cup creamy or chunky peanut butter

2 green onions, chopped

2 cloves garlic, peeled

2 tablespoons chopped fresh cilantro

2 tablespoons lime juice

1 tablespoon soy sauce

2 teaspoons granulated sugar

¼ teaspoon salt

⅛ to ¼ teaspoon cayenne pepper

4 boneless, skinless chicken breast halves, cut into 1-inch pieces (about 1 pound)

2 large red bell peppers, cut into 1-inch pieces

2 bunches green onions, cut into 1-inch pieces (white parts only)

30 (4-inch) skewers

PLACE pumpkin, milk, peanut butter, chopped green onions, garlic, cilantro, lime juice, soy sauce, sugar, salt and cayenne pepper in blender or food processor; cover. Blend until smooth. Combine ½ *cup* pumpkin mixture and chicken in medium bowl; cover. Marinate in refrigerator, stirring occasionally, for 1 hour.

ALTERNATELY thread chicken, bell peppers and green onion pieces onto skewers. Discard any remaining marinade. Grill or broil, turning once, for 10 minutes or until chicken is no longer pink. Heat *remaining* pumpkin mixture; serve with satay.

Makes about 30 appetizer servings

Note: If using wooden skewers, soak in water for 30 minutes before threading.

Swimming Rama

1¾ to 2 pounds fresh spinach, washed and stemmed *or* 2 packages
(10 ounces each) fresh spinach

3 boneless skinless chicken breasts (about 1¼ pounds), sliced crosswise
into ½-inch-wide strips

Peanut Sauce (recipe page 62)

1 fresh red chili pepper,* seeded and finely chopped *or* ¼ cup diced
red bell pepper

Marigold petals for garnish

*Chili peppers can sting and irritate the skin; wear rubber gloves when handling peppers and
do not touch eyes. Wash hands after handling.*

1. Set steamer basket in Dutch oven or large skillet; add water to within ¼ inch
of bottom of basket.

2. Bring water to a boil over high heat. Layer about ¼ of spinach in basket;
cover and steam 15 seconds. Quickly turn leaves over with tongs. Cover and
steam 15 seconds or until leaves are bright green and barely wilted.

3. Transfer spinach to colander. Repeat with remaining spinach. Lay spinach on
serving platter or individual plates.

4. Bring 6 cups water to a boil in large saucepan over high heat. Add chicken
to boiling water; remove saucepan from heat. Let stand, covered, 5 minutes or
until chicken is no longer pink in center.

5. Prepare Peanut Sauce.

6. Drain chicken; stir into hot Peanut Sauce and pour mixture over spinach.
Sprinkle with reserved chili pepper. Garnish, if desired.

Makes 4 servings

continued on page 62

Swimming Rama

Swimming Rama, continued

Peanut Sauce

    2 teaspoons vegetable oil
 ½ cup finely chopped onion
    3 cloves garlic, minced
 ½ cup chunky or creamy peanut butter
    3 tablespoons packed brown sugar
    2 tablespoons fish sauce
    1 teaspoon paprika
 ¼ teaspoon ground red pepper
    1 cup canned unsweetened coconut milk
    1 tablespoon cornstarch
    1 tablespoon water
    2 tablespoons lime juice

1. Heat oil in medium saucepan over medium-high heat. Add onion and garlic; cook and stir 2 to 3 minutes or until tender.

2. Reduce heat to medium. Add peanut butter, brown sugar, fish sauce, paprika and red pepper; stir until smooth. Slowly stir in coconut milk until well blended. (At this point, sauce may be cooled, covered and refrigerated up to 2 days in advance.)

3. Stir sauce constantly over medium heat until bubbling gently. Reduce heat to medium-low. Combine cornstarch and water in small cup; stir into sauce. Cook and stir 1 to 2 minutes or until sauce is thickened. Stir in lime juice.

Makes about 2 cups

Apricot Beef with Sesame Noodles

1 beef top sirloin steak (about 1 pound)
3 tablespoons Dijon mustard
3 tablespoons soy sauce
2 packages (3 ounces each) ramen noodles
2 tablespoons vegetable oil
2 cups (6 ounces) snow peas
1 medium red bell pepper, cut into cubes
¾ cup apricot preserves
½ cup beef broth
3 tablespoons chopped green onions
2 tablespoons toasted sesame seeds, divided

1. Cut beef lengthwise in half, then crosswise into ¼-inch strips. Combine beef, mustard and soy sauce in medium resealable food storage bag. Seal bag. Shake to evenly distribute marinade; refrigerate 4 hours or overnight.

2. Cook noodles according to package directions, omitting seasoning packets.

3. Heat oil in large skillet over medium-high heat. Add half of beef with marinade; stir-fry 2 minutes. Remove to bowl. Repeat with remaining beef and marinade. Return beef to skillet. Add snow peas and bell pepper; stir-fry 2 minutes. Add noodles, preserves, broth, green onions and 1 tablespoon sesame seeds. Cook 1 minute or until heated through. Top with remaining sesame seeds before serving.

Makes 4 to 6 servings

Kitchen How-To: Toast sesame seeds in a dry, heavy skillet over medium heat 2 minutes or until golden, stirring frequently.

Thai-Style Pork Kabobs

⅓ **cup soy sauce**
2 **tablespoons fresh lime juice**
2 **tablespoons water**
2 **teaspoons hot chili oil***
2 **cloves garlic, minced**
1 **teaspoon minced fresh ginger**
12 **ounces well-trimmed pork tenderloin**
1 **red or yellow bell pepper, cut into ½-inch pieces**
1 **red or sweet onion, cut into ½-inch chunks**
2 **cups hot cooked rice**

*If hot chili oil is not available, combine 2 teaspoons vegetable oil and ½ teaspoon red pepper flakes in small microwavable cup. Microwave at HIGH 30 to 45 seconds. Let stand 5 minutes to allow flavor to develop.

1. Combine soy sauce, lime juice, water, chili oil, garlic and ginger in medium bowl. Reserve ⅓ cup mixture for dipping sauce; set aside.

2. Cut pork tenderloin lengthwise in half; cut crosswise into 4-inch-thick slices. Cut slices into ½-inch strips. Add to bowl with soy sauce mixture; toss to coat. Cover; refrigerate at least 30 minutes or up to 2 hours, turning once.

3. To prevent sticking, spray grid with nonstick cooking spray. Prepare grill for direct cooking.

4. Remove pork from marinade; discard marinade. Alternately weave pork strips and thread bell pepper and onion chunks onto eight 8- to 10-inch metal skewers.

5. Grill, covered, over medium-hot coals 6 to 8 minutes or until pork is barely pink in center, turning halfway through grilling time. Serve with rice and reserved dipping sauce.

Makes 4 servings

Thai-Style Pork Kabobs

Satay Beef

1 pound beef tenderloin steaks
1 teaspoon cornstarch
5 tablespoons water, divided
3½ teaspoons soy sauce, divided
2 teaspoons dark sesame oil
2 tablespoons vegetable oil
1 medium yellow onion, coarsely chopped
1 clove garlic, minced
1 tablespoon dry sherry
1 tablespoon prepared satay sauce
1 teaspoon curry powder
½ teaspoon sugar

1. Cut meat crosswise into thin slices; flatten each slice by pressing with fingers.

2. Combine cornstarch, 3 tablespoons water, 1½ teaspoons soy sauce and sesame oil; mix well. Add to meat in medium bowl; stir to coat well. Let stand 20 minutes.

3. Heat vegetable oil in large skillet or wok over high heat. Add half of meat, spreading out slices so they don't overlap.

4. Cook meat slices 2 to 3 minutes on each side or just until lightly browned. Remove from skillet; set aside. Repeat with remaining meat slices.

5. Add onion and garlic to skillet; stir-fry about 3 minutes or until tender.

6. Combine remaining 2 tablespoons water, 2 teaspoons soy sauce, sherry, satay sauce, curry powder and sugar in small cup. Add to skillet; cook and stir until liquid boils. Return meat to skillet; cook and stir until heated.

Makes 4 servings

Satay Beef

Thai Satay Chicken Skewers

1 pound boneless skinless chicken breasts
⅓ cup soy sauce
2 tablespoons fresh lime juice
2 cloves garlic, minced
1 teaspoon grated fresh ginger
¾ teaspoon red pepper flakes
2 tablespoons water
¾ cup canned unsweetened coconut milk
1 tablespoon creamy peanut butter
4 green onions with tops, cut into 1-inch pieces

1. Cut chicken crosswise into ⅜-inch-wide strips; place in shallow glass dish.

2. Combine soy sauce, lime juice, garlic, ginger and red pepper flakes in small bowl. Reserve 3 tablespoons mixture. Add water to remaining mixture. Pour over chicken; toss to coat well. Cover; marinate in refrigerator at least 30 minutes or up to 2 hours, stirring mixture occasionally.

3. Soak 8 (10- to 12-inch) bamboo skewers 20 minutes in cold water to prevent them from burning; drain. Prepare grill for direct cooking.

4. Meanwhile, for peanut sauce, combine coconut milk, 3 tablespoons reserved soy sauce mixture and peanut butter in small saucepan. Bring to a boil over medium-high heat, stirring constantly. Reduce heat and simmer, uncovered, 2 to 4 minutes or until sauce thickens. Keep warm.

5. Drain chicken; reserve marinade. Weave 3 to 4 chicken strips accordion-style onto each skewer, alternating with green onion pieces. Brush chicken and onions with reserved marinade. Discard remaining marinade.

6. Place skewers on grid. Grill skewers on uncovered grill over medium-hot coals 6 to 8 minutes or until chicken is no longer pink, turning halfway through grilling time. Serve with warm peanut sauce for dipping.

Makes 4 servings

Thai Satay Chicken Skewers

Beef and Asparagus Stir-Fry

¾ **cup water**

3 **tablespoons soy sauce**

3 **tablespoons hoisin sauce**

1 **tablespoon cornstarch**

1 **tablespoon peanut or vegetable oil**

1 **pound sirloin steak, cut into thin strips**

1 **teaspoon dark sesame oil**

8 **shiitake mushrooms, stems removed and thinly sliced**

1 **cup baby corn**

8 **ounces asparagus (8 to 10 medium spears), cut into 1-inch pieces**

1 **cup sugar snap peas or snow peas**

1/2 **cup red bell pepper strips**

1/2 **cup cherry tomato halves (optional)**

1. Whisk together water, soy sauce, hoisin sauce and cornstarch in small bowl; set aside.

2. Heat peanut oil in large skillet or wok over medium-high heat. Add beef; cook and stir 5 to 6 minutes or until just slightly pink. Remove beef to plate with slotted spoon.

3. Add sesame oil, mushrooms and baby corn to skillet; cook and stir 2 to 3 minutes or until mushrooms are tender and corn is heated through. Add asparagus, snap peas and bell peppers; cook and stir 1 minute or until crisp-tender.

4. Return beef with any juices to skillet. Stir reserved soy sauce mixture and add to skillet; add tomatoes, if desired. Cook and stir 1 minute or until heated through and sauce has thickened.

Makes 4 servings

Beef and Asparagus Stir-Fry

From the Sea

*Thailand is surrounded by water and seafood is
a mainstay of the cuisine. Simply baked, steamed, or as part of a
stir-fry, fish takes on delicious new dimensions in Thai dishes.
Shrimp is a favorite, too, in specialties like Thai Shrimp Curry.*

Thai Shrimp Curry

1 can (14 ounces) unsweetened coconut milk, divided
1 teaspoon Thai red curry paste
1/3 cup water
1 tablespoon brown sugar
1 tablespoon fish sauce
  Peel of 1 lime, finely chopped
1 pound large raw shrimp, peeled and deveined
1/2 cup fresh basil leaves, thinly sliced
  Hot cooked jasmine rice
  Fresh pineapple wedges
1/2 cup unsalted peanuts

1. Pour half of coconut milk into large skillet. Bring to a boil over medium heat, stirring occasionally. Cook 5 to 6 minutes; oil may start to rise to surface. Stir in curry paste. Cook and stir 2 minutes.

2. Stir together remaining coconut milk and water. Add to skillet with brown sugar, fish sauce and lime peel. Cook over medium-low heat 10 to 15 minutes or until sauce thickens slightly.

3. Add shrimp and basil; reduce heat to low. Cook 3 to 5 minutes or until shrimp turn pink and opaque. Serve over jasmine rice; garnish with pineapple and peanuts.

Makes 4 servings

Thai Shrimp Curry

Thai-Style Tuna Steaks

2 tablespoons reduced-sodium soy sauce
2 teaspoons brown sugar
1 teaspoon ground cumin
1 teaspoon sesame oil or vegetable oil
¼ teaspoon crushed red pepper
1 clove garlic, minced
4 (4- to 5-ounce) tuna steaks
4 green onions, diagonally sliced
3 cups cooked white rice

MICROWAVE DIRECTIONS

Combine soy sauce, brown sugar, cumin, sesame oil, red pepper and garlic in a 11×7-inch microwave-safe baking dish. Add tuna and turn to coat both sides. Let marinate 5 to 15 minutes.

Turn tuna over and cover with lid or waxed paper. Microwave at HIGH (100% power) 1½ minutes, rotating dish ¼ turn. Sprinkle with green onions and continue to cook 1½ minutes longer or until tuna begins to flake easily when tested with a fork. Let stand, covered, 2 minutes. Serve tuna and sauce over rice.

Makes 4 servings

*Favorite recipe from **National Fisheries Institute***

Stir-Fried Catfish with Cucumber Rice

1 seedless cucumber

1¼ cups water

½ cup uncooked rice

4 green onions, thinly sliced

½ teaspoon white pepper

2 teaspoons canola oil

1 pound catfish fillets, cut into 1-inch chunks

1 teaspoon minced fresh ginger

1 clove garlic, minced

¼ teaspoon dark sesame oil

2 packages (6 ounces each) snow peas

1 red bell pepper, diced

¼ cup white wine or water

1 tablespoon cornstarch

1. Grate cucumber, on medium side of grater, into colander set over bowl to drain.

2. Combine water, rice, cucumber, green onions and white pepper in medium saucepan. Bring to a boil over medium heat. Cover; reduce heat to low. Cook about 20 minutes or until rice is tender and liquid is absorbed.

3. Heat oil in 12-inch nonstick skillet over high heat. Add catfish, ginger, garlic and sesame oil. Stir-fry 4 to 5 minutes or until catfish is just cooked. Add snow peas and bell pepper. Cover and cook 4 minutes.

4. Meanwhile, blend wine and cornstarch in small bowl. Pour over catfish mixture; cook and stir about 2 minutes or until sauce thickens. Serve over rice.

Makes 4 servings

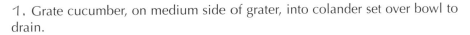

To round it out: Serve with egg drop soup, made by stirring beaten egg into simmering chicken broth seasoned with your favorite fresh chopped herbs, such as cilantro. Complete the meal with chilled fresh seasonal fruit cups or a scoop of lemon sorbet.

Baked Fish with Thai Pesto

1 lemon

4 green onions, sliced

1 piece (2 inches) fresh ginger, peeled and sliced

3 cloves garlic

1 to 2 jalapeño peppers, quartered

1½ cups lightly packed fresh basil leaves

1 cup lightly packed fresh cilantro leaves

¼ cup lightly packed fresh mint leaves

¼ cup roasted peanuts (salted or unsalted)

2 tablespoons sweetened shredded coconut

½ teaspoon sugar

½ cup peanut oil

2 pounds boneless fish fillets, such as salmon, halibut, cod or orange roughy (¾ inch thick)

Lemon and cucumber slices for garnish (optional)

1. To prepare pesto, grate peel of lemon; place in food processor. Juice lemon to measure 2 tablespoons. Add to food processor.

2. Add onions, ginger, garlic and jalapeño pepper to food processor. Process using on/off pulsing action until coarsely chopped.

3. Add basil, cilantro, mint, peanuts, coconut and sugar to food processor. With food processor running, slowly pour oil through feed tube until pesto is blended.

4. Preheat oven to 375°F. Rinse fish and pat dry with paper towels. Place fillets on lightly oiled baking sheet. Spread with pesto.

5. Bake 10 to 12 minutes or until fish flakes when tested with fork and is just opaque in center. Transfer fish to serving platter. Garnish, if desired.

Makes 4 to 6 servings

Baked Fish with Thai Pesto

Spicy Thai Shrimp Soup

1 tablespoon vegetable oil
1 pound medium raw shrimp, peeled and deveined, shells reserved
1 jalapeño pepper,* cut into slivers
1 tablespoon paprika
¼ teaspoon ground red pepper
4 cans (about 14 ounces each) chicken broth
  ½-inch strip *each* lemon and lime peel
1 can (15 ounces) straw mushrooms, drained
  Juice of 1 lemon
  Juice of 1 lime
2 tablespoons soy sauce
1 fresh red Thai chili pepper* *or* ¼ small red bell pepper, cut into slivers
¼ cup fresh cilantro leaves

Jalapeño peppers and thai chilies can sting and irritate the skin; wear rubber gloves when handling chilies and do not touch eyes. Wash hands after handling.

1. Heat wok over medium-high heat 1 minute. Drizzle oil into wok; heat 30 seconds. Add shrimp and jalapeño slivers; cook and stir 1 minute. Add paprika and ground red pepper. Stir-fry 1 minute more or until shrimp turn pink and opaque. Remove shrimp and jalapeño slivers to bowl; set aside.

2. Add shrimp shells to wok and stir-fry 30 seconds. Add chicken broth and lemon and lime peels; bring to a boil. Cover; reduce heat to low. Simmer 15 minutes.

3. Remove shells and peels from broth with slotted spoon; discard. Add mushrooms and shrimp mixture to broth; bring to a boil. Stir in lemon and lime juices, soy sauce and red pepper slivers. Ladle soup into bowls. Sprinkle with cilantro. Serve immediately.

Makes 8 first-course servings

Spicy Thai Shrimp Soup

Scallops, Shrimp and Squid with Basil and Chilies

8 ounces cleaned squid (body tubes, tentacles or a combination)
8 ounces scallops
8 to 12 ounces medium raw shrimp, peeled
¼ cup water
2 tablespoons oyster sauce
1 teaspoon cornstarch
1 tablespoon vegetable oil
6 to 8 jalapeño peppers,* seeded and thinly sliced
6 cloves garlic, minced
½ cup roasted peanuts, salted or unsalted
2 green onions, thinly sliced
½ cup slivered fresh basil leaves

*Jalapeño peppers can sting and irritate the skin; wear rubber gloves when handling peppers and do not touch eyes. Wash hands after handling.

1. Rinse squid; cut body tubes crosswise into ⅓-inch rings. Rinse and drain scallops. Slice large scallops crosswise into halves. Combine water, oyster sauce and cornstarch in small bowl; set aside.

2. To cook seafood, bring water to a boil in medium saucepan. Add shrimp; reduce heat to medium. Cook 2 to 3 minutes or until shrimp turn pink and opaque. Remove with slotted spoon to colander.

3. Return water to a boil. Add squid; reduce heat to medium. Cook rings 1 minute; cook tentacles 4 minutes. Remove to colander. Return water to a boil. Add scallops; reduce heat to medium. Cook 3 to 4 minutes or until opaque. Remove to colander.

4. Heat oil in wok or large skillet over medium-high heat. Add jalapeño peppers; cook and stir 3 minutes. Add garlic; cook and stir 2 minutes or until garlic is fragrant and peppers are tender.

5. Stir cornstarch mixture; add to wok. Cook and stir until bubbly. Add seafood, peanuts and green onions; cook and stir 2 to 3 minutes or until heated through. Stir in basil. Serve with rice.

Makes 4 servings

Scallops, Shrimp and Squid with Basil and Chilies

Noodles & Rice

Slurped at a roadside stand or enjoyed for breakfast, noodles and rice are served thousands of delightful ways in Thailand. Pad Thai (recipe on page 84), made with rice noodles, shrimp and chicken, is considered the national dish and is not to be missed.

Thai Chicken Noodles

2 tablespoons soy sauce

2 tablespoons water

1 tablespoon peanut butter

1 tablespoon honey

Juice of 1 lime

1 tablespoon minced ginger

2 cloves minced garlic

½ to 1 teaspoon red pepper flakes

1 tablespoon vegetable oil

4 boneless skinless chicken breasts (about 1 pound), cut into 1-inch pieces

1 cup snow pea pods

8 ounces uncooked linguine, cooked and drained

Chopped peanuts, fresh cilantro and lime wedges

1. Combine soy sauce, water, peanut butter, honey, lime juice, ginger, garlic and red pepper flakes in small microwavable bowl. Microwave on HIGH 30 seconds; whisk well.

2. Heat oil in large nonstick skillet or wok over medium-high heat. Cook and stir chicken 5 minutes or until cooked through. Add pea pods; cook and stir 4 minutes. Add cooked noodles and sauce to skillet; toss to combine. Cook until heated through. Garnish as desired.

Makes 4 to 5 servings

Thai Chicken Noodles

Pad Thai

8 ounces uncooked rice noodles, ⅛ inch wide

2 tablespoons rice wine vinegar

1½ tablespoons fish sauce

1 to 2 tablespoons fresh lemon juice

1 tablespoon ketchup

2 teaspoons sugar

¼ teaspoon red pepper flakes

1 tablespoon vegetable oil

1 boneless skinless chicken breast (about 4 ounces), finely chopped

2 green onions, thinly sliced

2 cloves garlic, minced

2 cups fresh bean sprouts

3 ounces small raw shrimp, peeled

¾ cup shredded red cabbage

1 medium carrot, shredded

3 tablespoons chopped fresh cilantro

2 tablespoons chopped unsalted dry-roasted peanuts

Lime wedges

1. Place noodles in medium bowl. Cover with lukewarm water; let stand 30 minutes or until soft. Drain and set aside. Combine rice wine vinegar, fish sauce, lemon juice, ketchup, sugar and red pepper flakes in small bowl.

2. Heat oil in wok or large nonstick skillet over medium-high heat. Add chicken, green onions and garlic. Cook and stir until chicken is no longer pink. Stir in noodles; cook 1 minute. Add bean sprouts and shrimp; cook just until shrimp turn pink and opaque, about 3 minutes. Stir in fish sauce mixture; toss to coat evenly. Cook until heated through, about 2 minutes.

3. Serve with shredded red cabbage, shredded carrot, chopped fresh cilantro, peanuts and lime wedges.

Makes 5 servings

Pad Thai

Lemon–Ginger Chicken with Puffed Rice Noodles

Vegetable oil for frying

4 ounces rice noodles, broken in half

3 boneless skinless chicken breasts, cut into 2½×1-inch strips

1 stalk lemongrass, outer leaves removed, cut into 1-inch pieces

3 cloves garlic, minced

1 teaspoon finely chopped fresh ginger

¼ teaspoon ground red pepper

¼ teaspoon black pepper

¼ cup water

1 tablespoon cornstarch

2 tablespoons peanut oil

6 ounces fresh snow peas, ends trimmed

1 can (8¾ ounces) baby corn, rinsed and drained

¼ cup chopped fresh cilantro

2 tablespoons packed brown sugar

2 tablespoons fish sauce

1 tablespoon soy sauce

1. Heat 3 inches vegetable oil in wok or Dutch oven until oil registers 375°F on deep-fry thermometer. Fry noodles in small batches 20 seconds or until puffy, holding down noodles in oil with slotted spoon to fry evenly. Drain on paper towels; set aside.

2. Combine chicken, lemongrass, garlic, ginger, red pepper and black pepper in medium bowl. Combine water and cornstarch in small bowl; set aside.

3. Heat wok over high heat 1 minute. Drizzle peanut oil into wok and heat 30 seconds. Add chicken mixture; stir-fry 3 minutes.

4. Add snow peas and baby corn; stir-fry 1 to 2 minutes. Stir cornstarch mixture; add to wok. Cook 1 minute or until thickened.

5. Add cilantro, brown sugar, fish sauce and soy sauce; cook until heated through. Remove and discard lemongrass. Serve over rice noodles.

Makes 4 servings

Lemon-Ginger Chicken with Puffed Rice Noodles

Rice Noodles with Broccoli and Tofu

1 package (14 ounces) firm or extra firm tofu
1 package (8 to 10 ounces) wide rice noodles
2 tablespoons peanut oil
3 medium shallots, thinly sliced
6 cloves garlic, minced
1 jalapeño pepper, minced
2 teaspoons minced fresh ginger
3 cups broccoli florets
3 tablespoons regular soy sauce
1 tablespoon sweet soy sauce (or substitute regular)
1 to 2 tablespoons fish sauce
Fresh basil leaves (optional)

1. Slice tofu horizontally into 2 pieces each about 1 inch thick. Place tofu on cutting board between layers of paper towels; put another cutting board on top and add a weight—a large can of vegetables works well—to press moisture out of tofu. Soak rice noodles in large bowl filled with warm water; let stand 30 minutes or until soft.

2. Meanwhile, heat oil in large skillet or wok. Cut tofu into bite-sized squares and blot dry. Stir-fry about 5 minutes or until tofu is speckled with light brown on all sides. Remove and reserve.

3. Add shallots, garlic, jalapeño and ginger to skillet. Stir-fry over medium-high heat 2 to 3 minutes; add broccoli and stir-fry to coat. Cover skillet; cook 3 minutes or until broccoli is crisp-tender.

4. Drain noodles well, add to skillet and stir to combine. Return tofu to skillet. Add soy sauces and fish sauce; stir-fry about 8 minutes or until noodles are coated and flavors blended. Taste and adjust seasoning. Serve with basil and with additional soy sauce, if desired.

Makes 4 to 6 servings

Rice Noodles with Broccoli and Tofu

Thai Meatballs and Noodles

Thai Meatballs (recipe follows)
12 ounces uncooked egg noodles
2 cans (about 14 ounces each) chicken broth
2 tablespoons packed brown sugar
2 tablespoons fish sauce or soy sauce
1 small piece fresh ginger (about 1×½ inch), cut into thin strips
1 medium carrot, cut into matchstick-size strips
1 pound bok choy, cut into ½-inch-wide strips
½ cup slivered fresh mint or basil leaves or chopped fresh cilantro

1. Prepare Thai Meatballs. While meatballs are cooking, cook noodles according to package directions; drain. Transfer noodles to large serving bowl; keep warm.

2. Heat chicken broth in large saucepan or wok over high heat. Add brown sugar, fish sauce and ginger; stir until sugar is dissolved. Add meatballs and carrot to saucepan; bring to a boil. Reduce heat to medium-low; cover and simmer 15 minutes or until meatballs are heated through.

3. Add bok choy; simmer 4 to 5 minutes or until stalks are crisp-tender. Stir in mint; spoon mixture over noodles in serving bowl. Garnish as desired.

Makes 6 servings

Thai Meatballs

1½ pounds ground beef or pork
¼ cup chopped fresh basil leaves
¼ cup chopped fresh mint leaves
2 tablespoons finely chopped fresh ginger
1 tablespoon fish sauce
6 cloves garlic, minced
1 teaspoon ground cinnamon
½ teaspoon fennel seeds, crushed
½ teaspoon black pepper
2 tablespoons peanut oil, divided

1. Combine beef, basil, mint, ginger, fish sauce, garlic, cinnamon, fennel and pepper in large bowl; mix until well blended. Rub cutting board with 1 tablespoon oil. Pat meat mixture into 12×8-inch rectangle on board. Cut into 32 squares. Shape each square into a ball.

2. Heat remaining 1 tablespoon oil in large skillet or wok over medium-high heat. Add meatballs in single layer; cook 8 to 10 minutes or until no longer pink in center, turning to brown all sides. (Cook in several batches.) Remove meatballs with slotted spoon to paper towels; drain.

Makes 32 meatballs

Thailand Peanut Pesto

  1 cup unsalted roasted peanuts
 ½ cup soy sauce
 ½ cup sesame oil
  1 teaspoon TABASCO® brand Pepper Sauce
 ¼ cup honey
 ⅓ cup water
  3 cloves garlic, minced
 12 ounces bow tie pasta, cooked according to package directions, drained
    Chopped green onions for garnish

Place peanuts in food processor; process until finely ground. With motor running, add soy sauce, sesame oil, TABASCO® Sauce, honey, water and garlic, one at a time, through feed tube. Process until a thick, smooth paste has formed. Transfer mixture to bowl; refrigerate, covered, until ready to use. Toss with bow tie pasta and garnish with chopped green onions.

Makes 4 servings

tip

Thai rice noodles are delicious and easy to handle. There is no need to cook the noodles, they are softened by a short soak in warm water (usually about 30 minutes). Don't soak them too long or make the water too hot, or the noodles will become soggy and lose their delightful texture.

Thai Fried Rice

2½ cups water

1⅓ cups long-grain white rice

8 ounces ground pork or pork sausage

1 tablespoon vegetable oil

1 medium onion, thinly sliced

1 tablespoon finely chopped fresh ginger

1 jalapeño pepper,* seeded and finely chopped

3 cloves garlic, minced

½ teaspoon ground turmeric or paprika

2 tablespoons fish sauce

2 cups chopped cooked vegetables such as broccoli, zucchini, red bell peppers, carrots, bok choy or spinach

3 eggs, lightly beaten

3 green onions, thinly sliced

½ cup fresh cilantro leaves

Jalapeños can sting and irritate the skin; wear rubber gloves when handling peppers and do not touch eyes. Wash hands after handling.

1. Bring water and rice to a boil in medium saucepan over high heat. Reduce heat to low; cover and simmer 20 minutes or until water is absorbed. Fluff rice with fork; let cool to room temperature. Cover and refrigerate until cold.

2. When rice is cold, cook pork in large skillet or wok over medium-high heat until no longer pink. Drain off excess fat; transfer pork to bowl.

3. Heat oil in skillet over medium-high heat. Add onion, ginger, jalapeño, garlic and turmeric; stir-fry until onion is tender. Stir in fish sauce; mix well. Stir in cold rice, vegetables and pork; cook and stir 3 to 4 minutes or until heated through.

4. Push rice mixture to side of wok and pour eggs into center. Cook eggs 2 to 3 minutes or just until set, lifting and stirring to scramble. Stir rice mixture into eggs.

5. Stir in green onions. Transfer to serving bowl; sprinkle with cilantro.

Makes 4 servings

Thai Fried Rice

Thai Curry Stir-Fry

½ **cup chicken broth**
2 **teaspoons cornstarch**
2 **teaspoons soy sauce**
1½ **teaspoons curry powder**
⅛ **teaspoon red pepper flakes**
   Nonstick olive oil cooking spray
3 **green onions, sliced**
2 **cloves garlic, minced**
2 **cups broccoli florets**
⅔ **cup sliced carrot**
1½ **teaspoons olive oil**
6 **ounces boneless skinless chicken breasts, cut into bite-size pieces**
⅔ **cup hot cooked rice**

1. Stir together broth, cornstarch, soy sauce, curry powder and red pepper flakes. Set aside.

2. Spray wok or large nonstick skillet with cooking spray. Heat over medium-high heat. Add green onions and garlic; stir-fry 1 minute. Remove from wok.

3. Add broccoli and carrot to wok; stir-fry 2 to 3 minutes or until crisp-tender. Remove from wok.

4. Add oil to hot wok. Add chicken and stir-fry 2 to 3 minutes or until no longer pink. Stir broth mixture; add to wok. Cook and stir until broth mixture comes to a boil and thickens slightly. Return all vegetables to wok. Heat through.

5. Serve with rice.

Makes 2 servings

Thai Curry Stir-Fry

Cellophane Noodle Salad

1 package (about 4 ounces) cellophane noodles*

2 tablespoons peanut or vegetable oil

8 ounces medium or large raw shrimp, peeled and deveined

3 cloves garlic, minced

¼ teaspoon red pepper flakes

½ cup cooked pork or ham strips (optional)

2 tablespoons soy sauce

1 tablespoon fresh lemon juice

1 tablespoon rice vinegar

1 tablespoon dark sesame oil

⅓ cup thinly sliced green onions or coarsely chopped fresh cilantro

*Cellophane noodles are available in the Asian section of most supermarkets. They are also called bean thread or glass noodles.

1. Place cellophane noodles in medium bowl; cover with warm water. Soak 15 minutes to soften. Drain well; cut into 2-inch pieces.

2. Meanwhile, heat wok or large skillet over medium-high heat. Add peanut oil; heat until hot. Add shrimp, garlic and red pepper flakes; stir-fry 2 minutes. Add pork, if desired, soy sauce, lemon juice, vinegar and sesame oil; stir-fry 1 minute.

3. Add cellophane noodles; stir-fry 1 minute or until heated through. Serve warm, chilled or at room temperature. Sprinkle with green onions before serving.

Makes 4 servings

Cellophane Noodle Salad

From Japan & Korea

Clean, fresh flavors are the hallmarks of Japanese and Korean food. Try Teriyaki Salmon with Asian Slaw or the classic Korean Broiled Beef (Bulgogi) for a dinnertime change of pace. With these recipes it's easy to experience a taste of Asia.

Teriyaki Salmon with Asian Slaw

4 tablespoons teriyaki sauce, divided

2 (5- to 6-ounce) boneless salmon fillets with skin (1 inch thick)

2½ cups packaged coleslaw mix

1 cup fresh or frozen snow peas, cut lengthwise into thin strips

½ cup thinly sliced radishes

2 tablespoons orange marmalade

1 teaspoon dark sesame oil

1. Preheat broiler or prepare grill for direct cooking. Spoon 2 tablespoons teriyaki sauce over meaty sides of salmon. Let stand while preparing vegetable mixture.

2. Combine coleslaw mix, snow peas and radishes in large bowl. Combine remaining 2 tablespoons teriyaki sauce, marmalade and sesame oil in small bowl. Add to coleslaw mixture; toss well.

3. Broil salmon 4 to 5 inches from heat source or grill, flesh side down, over medium coals without turning 6 to 10 minutes or until center is opaque. Transfer coleslaw mixture to serving plates; top with salmon.

Makes 2 servings

Teriyaki Salmon with Asian Slaw

Korean Beef Short Ribs

2½ pounds beef chuck flanken-style short ribs, cut ⅜ to ½ inch thick*
¼ cup water
¼ cup soy sauce
¼ cup chopped green onions
1 tablespoon sugar
2 teaspoons grated fresh ginger
2 teaspoons dark sesame oil
2 cloves garlic, minced
½ teaspoon black pepper
1 tablespoon sesame seeds, toasted

*Flanken-style ribs can be ordered from your butcher. They are cross-cut short ribs sawed through the bones, ⅜ to ½ inch thick.

1. Place ribs in large resealable food storage bag. Combine water, soy sauce, green onions, sugar, ginger, oil, garlic and pepper in small bowl; pour over ribs. Seal bag tightly, turning to coat. Marinate in refrigerator at least 4 hours or up to 24 hours, turning occasionally.

2. Prepare grill for direct cooking.

3. Drain ribs; reserve marinade. Place ribs on grid. Grill ribs, on covered grill, over medium-hot coals 5 minutes. Brush tops lightly with reserved marinade; turn and brush again. Discard remaining marinade. Continue to grill, covered, 5 to 6 minutes for medium or until desired doneness is reached. Sprinkle with sesame seeds.

Makes 4 to 6 servings

Korean Beef Short Ribs

Japanese Petal Salad

1 pound medium shrimp, cooked *or* 2 cups chicken, cooked and shredded
**   Romaine lettuce leaves**
2 fresh California Nectarines, halved, pitted and thinly sliced
2 cups sliced cucumber
2 celery stalks, cut into 3-inch matchstick pieces
⅓ cup shredded red radishes
**   Sesame Dressing (recipe follows) or low calorie dressing**
2 teaspoons sesame seeds (optional)

Center shrimp on 4 lettuce-lined salad plates. Fan nectarines to right side of shrimp; overlap cucumber slices to left side. Place celery at top of plate; mound radishes at bottom of plate. Prepare dressing; pour 3 tablespoons over each salad. Sprinkle with sesame seeds, if desired.

Makes 4 servings

Sesame Dressing: In small bowl, combine ½ cup rice wine vinegar (not seasoned type), 2 tablespoons reduced-sodium soy sauce, 2 teaspoons sugar and 2 teaspoons dark sesame oil. Stir until sugar is dissolved.

*Favorite recipe from **California Tree Fruit Agreement***

Japanese Petal Salad

Soba Stir-Fry

8 ounces uncooked soba noodles (Japanese buckwheat pasta)

1 tablespoon olive oil

2 cups sliced fresh shiitake mushrooms

1 medium red bell pepper, cut into thin strips

2 whole dried red chiles *or* ¼ teaspoon red pepper flakes

1 clove garlic, minced

2 cups shredded napa cabbage

½ cup chicken broth

2 tablespoons tamari or soy sauce

1 tablespoon rice wine or dry sherry

2 teaspoons cornstarch

1 package (14 ounces) firm tofu, drained and cut into 1-inch cubes

2 green onions, thinly sliced

1. Cook noodles according to package directions. Drain and set aside.

2. Heat oil in large nonstick skillet or wok over medium heat. Add mushrooms, bell pepper, dried chiles and garlic. Cook 3 minutes or until mushrooms are tender.

3. Add cabbage. Cover. Cook 2 minutes or until cabbage is wilted.

4. Combine chicken broth, tamari, rice wine and cornstarch in small bowl. Stir sauce into vegetable mixture. Cook 2 minutes or until sauce is bubbly.

5. Stir in tofu and noodles; toss gently until heated through. Sprinkle with green onions. Serve immediately.

Makes 4 servings

Soba Stir-Fry

Teriyaki Scallops

2 tablespoons soy sauce

1 tablespoon mirin* or sweet cooking rice wine

2 teaspoons sake or dry sherry

1 teaspoon sugar

1 pound large scallops

¼ teaspoon salt

8 ounces asparagus, diagonally sliced into 2-inch lengths

1 tablespoon vegetable oil

*Mirin is a Japanese sweet wine available in Japanese markets and the ethnic section of large supermarkets.

1. Combine soy sauce, mirin, sake and sugar in medium bowl; stir until sugar is dissolved. Add scallops; let stand 10 minutes, turning occasionally.

2. Meanwhile, bring 2½ cups water and salt to a boil in medium saucepan over high heat. Add asparagus; reduce heat to medium-high. Cook 3 to 5 minutes or until crisp-tender. Drain asparagus; keep warm.

3. Drain scallops, reserving marinade.

4. Preheat broiler. Line broiler pan with foil; brush broiler rack with vegetable oil. Place scallops on rack; brush lightly with marinade. Broil about 4 inches from heat source 4 to 5 minutes or until brown. Turn scallops with tongs; brush lightly with marinade. Broil 4 to 5 minutes or just until scallops are opaque in center. Serve immediately with asparagus. Garnish as desired.

Makes 4 servings

Teriyaki Scallops

Korean Broiled Beef (Bulgogi)

¼ **cup soy sauce**

2 **tablespoons Sesame Salt (recipe page 118)**

2 **tablespoons rice wine, beef broth or water**

1 **tablespoon sugar**

1 **tablespoon sesame oil**

¼ **teaspoon black pepper**

1 **boneless beef top sirloin steak (about 1½ pounds), cut into ⅛-inch-thick strips**

3 **green onions, thinly sliced**

2 **cloves garlic, minced**

   Leaf lettuce

   Cooked rice, roasted garlic, kimchee or Korean hot bean paste (optional)

1. Combine soy sauce, Sesame Salt, rice wine, sugar, sesame oil and pepper in large bowl. Add beef, green onions and garlic; toss to coat. Cover and refrigerate at least 30 minutes.

2. Preheat broiler. Spray broiler rack with nonstick cooking spray. Place strips of beef on broiler rack. Broil 4 inches from heat source 2 minutes; turn beef and broil 1 minute for medium or until desired doneness. (Beef can also be cooked to desired doneness on small hibachi.)

3. Line platter with leaf lettuce; arrange beef on top. Serve as is or use lettuce leaves to wrap beef with choice of accompaniments and eat burrito-style.

Makes 4 servings

Korean Broiled Beef (Bulgogi)

Asian Pesto Noodles

1 pound large raw shrimp, peeled and deveined
  Spicy Asian Pesto (recipe follows)
12 ounces uncooked soba (buckwheat) noodles

1. Marinate shrimp in ¾ cup pesto.

2. Cook soba noodles according to package directions; drain and set aside. Preheat broiler or grill.

3. Place marinated shrimp on metal skewers. (If using wooden skewers, soak skewers in bowl of water for at least 20 minutes before preparing recipe.) Place skewers under broiler or on grill; cook until shrimp are pink and opaque, about 3 minutes per side.

4. To serve, toss soba noodles with remaining pesto and place on platter. Top with shrimp skewers.

Makes 4 servings

Spicy Asian Pesto

  3 cups fresh basil leaves
  3 cups fresh cilantro leaves
  3 cups fresh mint leaves
  ¾ cup peanut oil
  3 tablespoons sugar
  2 to 3 tablespoons lime juice
  5 cloves garlic, chopped
  2 teaspoons fish sauce *or* 1 teaspoon salt
  1 serrano pepper,* finely chopped

*Serrano peppers can sting and irritate the skin; wear rubber gloves when handling peppers and do not touch eyes. Wash hands after handling.

Combine all pesto ingredients in blender or food processor; process until smooth.

Makes 2½ cups

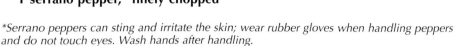

Orange Teriyaki Pork Packets

½ **pound lean pork stew meat (1-inch cubes)**
1½ **cups frozen bell pepper blend for stir-fry**
¼ **cup water chestnuts, coarsely chopped**
2 **sheets (18×12 inches) heavy-duty foil, lightly sprayed with nonstick cooking spray**
1 **tablespoon cornstarch**
2 **tablespoons teriyaki sauce**
2 **tablespoons orange marmalade**
½ **teaspoon dry mustard**
¼ **teaspoon ground ginger**
   Hot cooked rice

1. Preheat oven to 450°F.

2. Combine pork, pepper blend and water chestnuts in medium bowl; toss to mix. Place half of mixture on each foil sheet.

3. Dissolve cornstarch in teriyaki sauce. Stir in marmalade, mustard and ginger. Pour mixture over pork and vegetables.

4. Double fold sides and ends of foil to seal packets, leaving head space for heat circulation. Place packets on baking sheet.

5. Bake 20 to 23 minutes or until pork is tender. Remove from oven. Carefully open one end of each packet to allow steam to escape. Open packets and transfer contents to serving plates. Serve with rice.

Makes 2 servings

tip

Teriyaki sauce is made from soy sauce, sugar, sake or rice wine and other seasonings. In Japanese the word comes from "teri" which means sheen and "yaki" which means grill or broil. The sugar in teriyaki sauce creates a light glaze or sheen that makes food look as appetizing as it tastes. Don't limit teriyaki sauce to Japanese cuisine. It is an excellent baste or marinade for any grilled meat or vegetable.

Japanese Yakitori

1 pound boneless skinless chicken breasts, cut into ¾-inch-wide strips
2 tablespoons sherry or pineapple juice
2 tablespoons soy sauce
1 tablespoon sugar
1 tablespoon peanut oil
½ teaspoon minced garlic
½ teaspoon minced ginger
5 ounces red pearl onions
½ fresh pineapple, cut into 1-inch wedges

1. Place chicken in large resealable food storage bag. Combine sherry, soy sauce, sugar, oil, garlic and ginger in small bowl; mix thoroughly to dissolve sugar. Pour into plastic bag with chicken; seal bag and turn to coat thoroughly. Refrigerate 30 minutes or up to 2 hours, turning occasionally. (If using wooden or bamboo skewers, soak them in water 30 minutes to keep from burning.)

2. Meanwhile, place onions in boiling water for 4 minutes; drain and cool in ice water to stop cooking. Cut off root ends and slip off outer skins; set aside.

3. Drain chicken, reserving marinade. Weave chicken accordion-style onto skewers, alternating onions and pineapple with chicken. Brush with reserved marinade; discard remaining marinade.

4. Grill on uncovered grill over medium-hot coals 6 to 8 minutes or until chicken is cooked through, turning once.

Makes 6 servings

Japanese Yakitori

Braised Eggplant in Garlic Sauce

1 medium eggplant (1¼ pounds), peeled and cut into chunks
1 teaspoon salt
2 tablespoons soy sauce
1 tablespoon rice vinegar or white vinegar
1 tablespoon rice wine or dry sherry
1 tablespoon dark sesame oil
2 teaspoons cornstarch
2 teaspoons sugar
2 tablespoons vegetable oil
2 cloves garlic, minced
¼ cup chicken broth
1 small red bell pepper, cut into strips
1 green onion, cut into 1-inch pieces

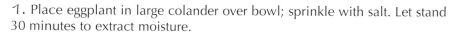

1. Place eggplant in large colander over bowl; sprinkle with salt. Let stand 30 minutes to extract moisture.

2. Combine soy sauce, vinegar, rice wine, sesame oil, cornstarch and sugar in cup; mix well. Set aside.

3. Rinse eggplant with cold water; pat dry with paper towels. Heat wok over high heat about 1 minute. Drizzle vegetable oil into wok; heat 15 seconds. Add eggplant and stir-fry about 5 minutes or until lightly browned. Add garlic; stir-fry 15 seconds.

4. Add chicken broth to wok; cover and reduce heat to medium. Cook eggplant 3 minutes.

5. Uncover wok. Increase heat to medium-high. Add bell pepper and green onion; stir-fry 2 minutes. Stir cornstarch mixture; add to wok. Cook and stir until liquid boils and thickens. Transfer to warm serving dish.

Makes 6 servings

Braised Eggplant in Garlic Sauce

Grilled Swordfish with Hot Red Sauce

2 to 3 green onions
2 tablespoons Sesame Salt (recipe page 118)
4 swordfish or halibut steaks (about 1½ pounds total)
2 tablespoons hot bean paste*
2 tablespoons soy sauce
4 teaspoons sugar
1 tablespoon dark sesame oil
4 cloves garlic, minced
⅛ teaspoon black pepper

*Available in specialty stores or Asian markets.

1. Spray grid of grill or broiler rack with nonstick cooking spray. Prepare coals for grilling or preheat broiler.

2. Cut off and discard root ends of green onions. Finely chop enough green onions to measure ¼ cup; set aside. Prepare Sesame Salt; set aside.

3. Rinse swordfish and pat dry with paper towels. Place in shallow glass dish.

4. Combine green onions, Sesame Salt, hot bean paste, soy sauce, sugar, sesame oil, garlic and pepper in small bowl; mix well.

5. Spread half of marinade over fish; turn fish over and spread with remaining marinade. Cover with plastic wrap and refrigerate 30 minutes.

6. Remove fish from marinade; discard remaining marinade. Place fish on prepared grid. Grill fish over medium-hot coals or broil 4 to 5 minutes per side or until fish is opaque. Garnish as desired.

Makes 4 servings

continued on page 118

Grilled Swordfish with Hot Red Sauce

Grilled Swordfish with Hot Red Sauce, continued

Sesame Salt

½ cup sesame seeds
¼ teaspoon salt

To toast sesame seeds, heat small skillet over medium heat. Add sesame seeds; cook and stir about 5 minutes or until seeds are golden. Cool. Crush sesame seeds and salt with mortar and pestle or process in clean coffee or spice grinder. Refrigerate in covered glass jar.

Wasabi Salmon

2 tablespoons soy sauce
**1½ teaspoons wasabi paste or wasabi prepared from powder, divided, plus
   more to taste**
4 salmon fillets (6 ounces each), with skin
¼ cup mayonnaise

1. Preheat broiler. Combine soy sauce and ½ teaspoon wasabi paste; mix well. Spoon mixture over salmon. Place salmon, skin sides down, on grid over medium coals or rack of broiler pan. Grill or broil 4 to 5 inches from heat source 8 minutes or until salmon is opaque in center.

2. Meanwhile, combine mayonnaise and remaining 1 teaspoon wasabi paste; mix well. Taste and add more wasabi, if desired. Transfer salmon to serving plates; top with mayonnaise mixture.

Makes 4 servings

Wasabi is sometimes referred to as Japanese horseradish. It has a fiery flavor and is the green paste usually served with sushi. Wasabi is available in a powdered form, which must be mixed with water to form a paste, or in a squeezable tube, which is ready to use. You'll find wasabi powder in the Asian section of most large supermarkets.

Wok Sukiyaki

 1 package (3¾ ounces) cellophane noodles (bean threads)
 ½ cup beef broth
 ½ cup teriyaki sauce
 ¼ cup sake, rice wine or dry sherry
 1 tablespoon sugar
 1 pound beef tenderloin or top sirloin steaks
 2 tablespoons vegetable oil, divided
12 fresh shiitake or button mushrooms (about 6 ounces), stems removed
 ½ pound firm tofu, drained and cut into 1-inch cubes
 6 green onions with tops, cut into 2-inch pieces
 ½ pound fresh spinach, stems removed

1. Place noodles in bowl; cover with water. Let stand 30 minutes or until softened; drain. Cut into 4-inch lengths; set aside.

2. Combine beef broth, teriyaki sauce, sake and sugar in small bowl; mix well. Set aside. Cut beef crosswise into ¼-inch strips.

3. Heat wok over high heat 1 minute. Drizzle 1 tablespoon oil into wok and heat 30 seconds. Add half of beef; stir-fry 3 minutes or until browned. Remove to bowl; set aside. Repeat with remaining 1 tablespoon oil and beef.

4. Reduce heat to medium. Add mushrooms to wok; stir-fry 1 minute and move to one side of wok. Add tofu to bottom of wok; fry 1 minute, stirring gently. Move to another side of wok. Add green onions to bottom of wok. Add broth mixture and bring to a boil. Move onions up side of wok.

5. Add noodles and spinach, keeping each in separate piles and stirring gently to soften in teriyaki sauce. Push up side of wok. Add beef and any juices; heat through.

6. Place wok on table over wok ring stand or trivet.

Makes 4 servings

Teriyaki Steak with Onions and Mushrooms

1 boneless beef sirloin steak, about 1 inch thick (1½ pounds)
¾ cup light teriyaki sauce, divided
1 tablespoon vegetable oil
1 can (8 ounces) sliced mushrooms, drained
1 small red or green bell pepper, cut into strips
1⅓ cups *French's®* French Fried Onions, divided

1. Brush each side of steak with 1 tablespoon teriyaki sauce. Heat oil in grill pan or heavy skillet over medium-high heat. Cook steak for 3 to 4 minutes per side or until desired doneness. Remove steak; keep warm.

2. Add mushrooms and bell pepper to pan; cook until pepper is crisp-tender. Stir in remaining teriyaki sauce and *⅔ cup* French Fried Onions; heat through.

3. Serve mushroom mixture over steak. Sprinkle with remaining onions.

Makes 6 servings

Prep Time: 5 minutes
Cook Time: 15 minutes

Teriyaki Steak with Onions and Mushrooms

Japanese-Style Steak with Garden Sunomono

GARDEN SUNOMONO

1 medium cucumber, peeled, seeded and thinly sliced

½ teaspoon salt

¼ cup rice wine vinegar

3 tablespoons sugar

1 cup thinly sliced radishes

½ cup shredded carrot

JAPANESE-STYLE STEAK

3 New York strip steaks, ¾ inch thick (8 ounces each)

¼ cup soy sauce

3 tablespoons dry sherry

1 teaspoon dark sesame oil

½ teaspoon ground ginger

1 large clove garlic, minced

1. For sunomono, place cucumber in colander; sprinkle with salt. Let stand 20 minutes. Press out excess liquid; rinse with water. Press again.

2. Blend vinegar and sugar in medium bowl, stirring until sugar dissolves. Add cucumber, radishes and carrot. Cover; refrigerate 30 minutes to 2 hours, stirring occasionally.

3. Place steaks in shallow baking dish. Blend soy sauce, sherry, sesame oil, ginger and garlic in small bowl; pour over steaks. Cover; refrigerate 30 minutes to 2 hours, turning steaks occasionally.

4. Preheat broiler. Remove steaks from marinade; place on broiler pan rack. Discard marinade. Broil 2 to 3 inches from heat 5 to 6 minutes per side or until desired doneness.

5. Transfer steaks to cutting board; slice across grain into ½-inch slices. Serve with sunomono.

Makes 4 servings

Japanese-Style Steak with Garden Sunomono

Chicken Teriyaki

8 large chicken drumsticks (about 2 pounds)
⅓ cup teriyaki sauce
2 tablespoons brandy or apple juice
1 green onion, minced
1 tablespoon vegetable oil
1 teaspoon ground ginger
½ teaspoon sugar
¼ teaspoon garlic powder
Prepared sweet and sour sauce (optional)

1. Remove skin from drumsticks, if desired, by pulling skin toward end of leg using paper towel; discard skin.

2. Place chicken in large resealable food storage bag. Combine teriyaki sauce, brandy, green onion, oil, ginger, sugar and garlic powder in small bowl; pour over chicken. Close bag securely, turning to coat. Marinate in refrigerator at least 1 hour or overnight, turning occasionally.

3. Prepare grill for indirect cooking.

4. Drain chicken; reserve marinade. Place chicken on grid directly over drip pan. Grill, covered, over medium-high heat 60 minutes or until chicken is cooked through (180°F), turning and brushing with reserved marinade every 20 minutes. *Do not brush with marinade during last 5 minutes of grilling.* Discard remaining marinade. Serve with sweet and sour sauce, if desired.

Makes 4 servings

Chicken Teriyaki

From China

Everybody loves Chinese food, and with these recipes
you don't have to order out to enjoy your favorites.
From Kung Pao Chicken to exotic Chicken with Lychees, there
are plenty of dishes to explore. Get your chopsticks ready!

Shrimp and Vegetables with Lo Mein Noodles

2 tablespoons vegetable oil

1 pound medium raw shrimp, peeled

2 packages (21 ounces each) frozen lo mein stir-fry mix
with sauce

1 small wedge cabbage

¼ cup peanuts, chopped

2 tablespoons chopped fresh cilantro

1. Heat oil in wok or large skillet over medium-high heat. Add shrimp; stir-fry 3 minutes or until shrimp are pink and opaque. Remove shrimp from wok to medium bowl. Set aside.

2. Remove sauce packet from stir-fry mix. Add frozen vegetables and noodles to wok; stir in sauce. Cover and cook 7 to 8 minutes, stirring frequently.

3. While vegetable mixture is cooking, shred cabbage.

4. Stir shrimp into vegetable mixture; heat through. Sprinkle with peanuts and cilantro. Serve with cabbage.

Makes 6 servings

Prep and Cook Time: 20 minutes

Shrimp and Vegetables with Lo Mein Noodles

Buddha's Delight

1 package (1 ounce) dried shiitake or black Chinese mushrooms

1 package (about 12 ounces) firm tofu, drained

1 tablespoon peanut or vegetable oil

2 cups diagonally cut 1-inch asparagus pieces *or* 1 package (10 ounces) frozen cut asparagus, thawed and drained

1 medium onion, cut into thin wedges

2 cloves garlic, minced

½ cup chicken broth

3 tablespoons hoisin sauce

¼ cup coarsely chopped fresh cilantro or thinly sliced green onions

1. Place mushrooms in small bowl; cover with warm water. Soak 20 minutes to soften. Drain over fine strainer, squeezing out excess water into measuring cup; reserve. Discard mushroom stems; slice caps.

2. Press tofu lightly between paper towels; cut into ³/₄-inch squares or triangles.

3. Heat wok or large skillet over medium-high heat. Add oil; heat until hot. Add asparagus, onion wedges and garlic; stir-fry 4 minutes for fresh or 3 minutes for frozen asparagus.

4. Add mushrooms, ¼ cup reserved mushroom liquid,* broth and hoisin sauce. Reduce heat to medium-low. Simmer, uncovered, until asparagus is crisp-tender, 2 to 3 minutes for fresh or 1 minute for frozen asparagus.

5. Stir in tofu; heat through, stirring occasionally. Ladle into shallow bowls. Sprinkle with cilantro.

Makes 2 main-dish or 4 side-dish servings

*Remaining mushroom liquid may be covered and refrigerated up to 3 days or frozen up to 3 months. It may be used in soups and stews.

Buddha's Delight

Fried Green Beans

4 ounces lean ground pork or turkey

2 tablespoons plus 1 teaspoon soy sauce, divided

2 tablespoons plus 1 teaspoon rice wine or dry sherry, divided

½ teaspoon sesame oil

2 tablespoons water

1 teaspoon sugar

3 cups vegetable oil

1 pound fresh green beans, trimmed and cut into 2-inch lengths

1 tablespoon sliced green onion (white part only)

1. Combine pork, 1 teaspoon soy sauce, 1 teaspoon rice wine and sesame oil in medium bowl; mix well. Set aside.

2. Combine water, sugar, remaining 2 tablespoons soy sauce and 2 tablespoons rice wine in small bowl; mix well. Set aside.

3. Heat vegetable oil in wok over medium-high heat until oil registers 375°F on deep-fry thermometer. Carefully add ½ of beans and fry 2 to 3 minutes or until beans blister and are crisp-tender. Remove beans with slotted spoon to paper towels; drain. When oil returns to 375°F, repeat with remaining beans.

4. Pour off oil; heat wok over medium-high heat 30 seconds. Add pork mixture and stir-fry about 2 minutes or until well browned. Add beans and soy sauce mixture; toss until heated through. Transfer to serving dish. Sprinkle with green onion.

Makes 4 servings

Fried Green Beans

Mandarin Orange Chicken

2 tablespoons rice vinegar

2 tablespoons soy sauce

2 tablespoons olive oil, divided

2 teaspoons grated orange peel

1 clove garlic, minced

1 pound boneless skinless chicken breasts, cut into strips

2 cans (11 ounces each) mandarin oranges, undrained

½ cup (approximately) orange juice

2 tablespoons cornstarch

½ teaspoon red pepper flakes

1 onion, cut into thin wedges

1 small zucchini, sliced

1 red bell pepper, cut into 1-inch triangles

1 can (3 ounces) chow mein noodles (optional)

1. Combine vinegar, soy sauce, 1 tablespoon oil, orange peel and garlic in medium bowl. Add chicken; toss to coat well. Cover and refrigerate 15 minutes to 1 hour.

2. Drain chicken, reserving marinade. Drain oranges, reserving liquid; set oranges aside. Combine marinade from chicken and liquid from oranges in small bowl; add enough orange juice to make 2 cups liquid. Whisk in cornstarch and red pepper flakes; set aside.

3. Heat remaining 1 tablespoon oil in wok or large skillet over high heat. Add chicken; stir-fry 2 to 3 minutes or until cooked through. Remove chicken; set aside.

4. Stir-fry onion 1 minute over high heat. Add zucchini; stir-fry 1 minute. Add bell pepper; stir-fry 1 minute or until all vegetables are crisp-tender. Add orange juice mixture. Cook and stir until mixture comes to a boil; boil 1 minute. Add chicken; cook until hot. Add oranges and gently stir. Transfer to serving plate. Top with chow mein noodles, if desired.

Makes 6 servings

Mandarin Orange Chicken

Hot and Sour Shrimp

½ **package (½ ounce) dried shiitake or black Chinese mushrooms***
½ **small unpeeled cucumber**
1 **tablespoon brown sugar**
2 **teaspoons cornstarch**
3 **tablespoons rice vinegar**
2 **tablespoons soy sauce**
1 **tablespoon vegetable oil**
1 **pound medium raw shrimp, peeled and deveined**
2 **cloves garlic, minced**
¼ **teaspoon red pepper flakes**
1 **large red bell pepper, cut into short, thin strips**
   Hot cooked Chinese egg noodles (optional)

Or substitute ¾ cup sliced fresh mushrooms. Omit step 1.

1. Place mushrooms in small bowl; cover with warm water. Soak 20 minutes to soften. Drain; squeeze out excess water. Discard stems; slice caps.

2. Cut cucumber in half lengthwise; scrape out seeds. Slice crosswise.

3. Combine brown sugar and cornstarch in small bowl. Blend in vinegar and soy sauce until smooth.

4. Heat oil in wok or large nonstick skillet over medium heat. Add shrimp, garlic and red pepper flakes; stir-fry 1 minute. Add mushrooms and bell pepper strips; stir-fry 2 minutes or until shrimp are pink and opaque.

5. Stir vinegar mixture; add to wok. Cook and stir 30 seconds or until sauce boils and thickens. Add cucumber; stir-fry until heated through. Serve over noodles, if desired.

Makes 4 servings

Hot and Sour Shrimp

Asparagus Chicken with Black Bean Sauce

5 teaspoons cornstarch, divided
4 teaspoons soy sauce, divided
1 tablespoon dry sherry
1 teaspoon sesame oil
3 boneless skinless chicken breasts, cut into bite-size pieces
1 tablespoon fermented, salted black beans*
1 teaspoon minced fresh ginger
1 clove garlic, minced
½ cup chicken broth
1 tablespoon oyster sauce
1 medium yellow onion
3 tablespoons vegetable oil, divided
1 pound fresh asparagus spears, trimmed and diagonally cut into 1-inch pieces
2 tablespoons water

*Fermented black beans (soy beans) are available in Asian markets. 1 tablespoon prepared Chinese black bean sauce may be substituted. If using prepared sauce, skip rinsing beans and combine sauce with ginger and garlic.

1. For marinade, combine 2 teaspoons cornstarch, 2 teaspoons soy sauce, sherry and sesame oil in large bowl; mix well. Add chicken; stir to coat well. Let stand 30 minutes.

2. Place black beans in sieve; rinse under cold running water. Finely chop beans. Combine with ginger and garlic; set aside.

3. Combine remaining 3 teaspoons cornstarch, remaining 2 teaspoons soy sauce, chicken broth and oyster sauce in small bowl; mix well. Set aside.

4. Peel onion; cut into eight wedges. Separate wedges; set aside.

5. Heat 2 tablespoons vegetable oil in wok or large skillet over high heat. Add chicken; stir-fry until cooked through, about 3 minutes. Remove from wok; set aside.

continued on page 138

Asparagus Chicken with Black Bean Sauce

Asparagus Chicken with Black Bean Sauce, continued

6. Heat remaining 1 tablespoon vegetable oil in wok. Add onion and asparagus; stir-fry 30 seconds.

7. Add water; cover. Cook, stirring occasionally, until asparagus is crisp-tender, about 2 minutes. Return chicken to wok.

8. Stir chicken broth mixture; add to wok with black bean mixture. Cook until sauce boils and thickens, stirring constantly. Garnish, if desired.

Makes 3 to 4 servings

Easy Fried Rice

¼ cup BERTOLLI® Olive Oil
4 cups cooked rice
2 cloves garlic, finely chopped
1 envelope LIPTON® RECIPE SECRETS® Onion Mushroom Soup Mix
½ cup water
1 tablespoon soy sauce
1 cup frozen peas and carrots, partially thawed
2 eggs, lightly beaten

1. In 12-inch nonstick skillet, heat oil over medium-high heat and cook rice, stirring constantly, 2 minutes or until rice is heated through. Stir in garlic.

2. Stir in soup mix blended with water and soy sauce and cook 1 minute. Stir in peas and carrots and cook 2 minutes or until heated through.

3. Make a well in center of rice and quickly stir in eggs until cooked.

Makes 4 servings

Prep Time: 10 minutes
Cook Time: 10 minutes

Beijing Fillet of Sole

2 tablespoons soy sauce

2 teaspoons dark sesame oil

4 sole fillets (6 ounces each)

1¼ cups preshredded cabbage or coleslaw mix

½ cup crushed chow mein noodles

1 egg white, lightly beaten

2 teaspoons sesame seeds

1 package (10 ounces) frozen snow peas, cooked and drained

1. Preheat oven to 350°F. Combine soy sauce and oil in small bowl. Place sole in shallow dish. Lightly brush both sides of sole with soy sauce mixture.

2. Combine cabbage, noodles, egg white and remaining soy sauce mixture in small bowl. Spoon evenly over each fillet. Roll up fillets. Place, seam side down, in shallow foil-lined roasting pan.

3. Sprinkle rolls with sesame seeds. Bake 25 to 30 minutes or until fish flakes when tested with fork. Serve with snow peas.

Makes 4 servings

tip

"Mein" are Chinese wheat noodles and are available in many forms. The canned chow mein noodles used in Americanized dishes, such as Chinese chicken salad and the recipe above, have been fried to make them crisp. Don't confuse them with other dried and fresh forms of wheat noodles which are also called chow mein. Lo mein refers to a dish of boiled noodles stir-fried with meat and vegetables.

Broiled Hunan Fish Fillets

3 tablespoons soy sauce
1 tablespoon finely chopped green onion
2 teaspoons dark sesame oil
1 clove garlic, minced
1 teaspoon minced fresh ginger
¼ teaspoon red pepper flakes
   Nonstick cooking spray
1 pound red snapper, scrod or cod fillets

1. Combine soy sauce, green onion, oil, garlic, ginger and red pepper flakes in small bowl.

2. Spray rack of broiler pan with nonstick cooking spray. Place fish on rack; brush with soy sauce mixture.

3. Broil 4 to 5 inches from heat 10 minutes or until fish flakes when tested with fork. Serve on lettuce-lined plate, if desired.

Makes 4 servings

Instead of broiling or grilling fish fillets, try steaming them. This method is often used in Chinese recipes. The fish is seasoned and sometimes wrapped in lettuce leaves or placed on vegetables, then cooked in a bamboo steamer. You can still try this method if you don't have a steamer. Place a wire rack over at least an inch of water in a wok or large skillet. The water should not touch the rack. Place the seasoned fish on a shallow heatproof plate that will fit on the rack. Bring the water to a boil; place the plate on the rack. Cover and reduce the heat to medium. Steam a 1-inch fish fillet about 10 minutes, or until it flakes when tested with a fork.

Broiled Hunan Fish Fillets

Hong Kong Fried Rice Cakes

1 box (about 6 ounces) chicken-flavored rice mix
1/2 cup sliced green onions
2 eggs, beaten
2 tablespoons chopped fresh parsley
1 tablespoon hoisin sauce
1 tablespoon soy sauce
1 teaspoon minced fresh ginger
1 clove garlic, minced
2 to 3 tablespoons vegetable oil, divided

1. Prepare rice according to package directions, omitting butter. Cover and refrigerate one hour or until completely chilled. Add remaining ingredients, except oil, to rice; mix well. Form rice mixture into cakes, 3 inches in diameter.

2. Heat 1 tablespoon oil in large skillet over medium heat. Cook 4 cakes at a time 3 to 4 minutes on each side or until golden brown. Add additional oil to skillet as needed.

Makes 4 to 6 servings

tip

Soy sauce is made by fermenting boiled soybeans and roasted wheat or barley. While Americans are familiar with only one kind, a trip to any Asian store will reveal that there are dozens of varieties available, including mushroom soy sauce, sweet soy sauce, tamari soy sauce and many others. To choose a good quality soy sauce, check the label for the words "naturally fermented." The ingredients list should not include artificial colors or flavors.

Hong Kong Fried Rice Cakes

Chicken with Lychees

3 boneless skinless chicken breasts (about 1 pound)
¼ cup plus 1 teaspoon cornstarch, divided
½ cup water, divided
½ cup tomato sauce
1 teaspoon sugar
1 teaspoon instant chicken bouillon granules
3 tablespoons vegetable oil
6 green onions with tops, cut into 1-inch pieces
1 red bell pepper, cut into 1-inch pieces
1 can (11 ounces) whole peeled lychees, drained
Cooked cellophane noodles (bean threads)

1. Cut chicken into bite-size pieces.

2. Place ¼ cup cornstarch in large resealable food storage bag; add chicken pieces. Seal bag; shake until chicken is well coated; set aside.

3. Combine remaining 1 teaspoon cornstarch and ¼ cup water in small cup; mix well. Set aside.

4. Combine remaining ¼ cup water, tomato sauce, sugar and bouillon granules in small bowl; mix well. Set aside.

5. Heat oil in wok or large skillet over high heat. Add chicken; stir-fry until lightly browned, 5 to 8 minutes. Add onions and bell pepper; stir-fry 1 minute.

6. Pour tomato sauce mixture over chicken mixture. Stir in lychees. Reduce heat to low; cover. Simmer until chicken is tender and cooked through, about 5 minutes.

7. Stir cornstarch mixture; add to wok. Cook and stir until sauce boils and thickens. Serve over hot cellophane noodles.

Makes 4 servings

Chicken with Lychees

Chinese Crab & Cucumber Salad

1 large cucumber, peeled
12 ounces fresh pasteurized or thawed frozen crabmeat, flaked
½ red bell pepper, diced
½ cup mayonnaise
3 tablespoons soy sauce
1 tablespoon sesame oil
1 teaspoon ground ginger
½ pound bean sprouts
1 tablespoon sesame seeds, toasted
Fresh chives, cut into 1-inch pieces

Cut cucumber in half lengthwise; scoop out seeds. Cut cucumber into 1-inch pieces. Combine cucumber, crabmeat and bell pepper in large bowl. Blend mayonnaise, soy sauce, sesame oil and ginger in small bowl. Pour over crabmeat mixture; toss to mix well. Refrigerate 1 hour to allow flavors to blend. To serve, arrange bean sprouts on individual serving plates. Spoon crabmeat mixture on top; sprinkle with sesame seeds and chives.

Makes 4 main-dish servings

Pasteurized crabmeat has been heat treated and sealed in an air-tight container so that it keeps fresh significantly longer than fresh crab as long as it is unopened and under refrigeration. Once the can has been opened, the contents should be used within 3 days. Both pasteurized crabmeat and frozen crabmeat are available at seafood markets and at the fish counter of some supermarkets. Fresh or canned crabmeat may be substituted.

Szechwan Beef Lo Mein

1 boneless beef top sirloin steak (about 1 pound)

4 cloves garlic, minced

2 teaspoons minced fresh ginger

¾ teaspoon red pepper flakes, divided

1 tablespoon vegetable oil

1 can (about 14 ounces) vegetable broth

1 cup water

2 tablespoons soy sauce

1 package (8 ounces) frozen mixed vegetables for stir-fry

1 package (9 ounces) refrigerated angel hair pasta

¼ cup chopped fresh cilantro (optional)

1. Cut steak lengthwise in half, then crosswise into thin slices. Toss steak with garlic, ginger and ½ teaspoon red pepper flakes.

2. Heat oil in large nonstick skillet over medium-high heat. Add half of beef to skillet; stir-fry 2 minutes or until meat is barely pink in center. Remove from skillet; set aside. Repeat with remaining beef.

3. Add vegetable broth, water, soy sauce and remaining ¼ teaspoon red pepper flakes to skillet; bring to a boil over high heat. Add vegetables; return to a boil. Reduce heat to low; simmer, covered, 3 minutes or until vegetables are crisp-tender.

4. Uncover; stir in pasta. Return to a boil over high heat. Reduce heat to medium; simmer, uncovered, 2 minutes, separating pasta with two forks. Return steak and any accumulated juices to skillet; simmer 1 minute or until pasta is tender and steak is hot. Sprinkle with cilantro, if desired.

Makes 4 servings

Simmering Hot & Sour Soup

2 cans (14½ ounces each) chicken broth

1 cup chopped cooked chicken or pork

4 ounces fresh shiitake mushroom caps, thinly sliced

½ cup sliced bamboo shoots, cut into thin strips

3 tablespoons rice vinegar or rice wine vinegar

2 tablespoons soy sauce

1½ teaspoons Chinese chili paste *or* 1 teaspoon hot chili oil

4 ounces firm tofu, well drained and cut into ½-inch pieces

2 teaspoons dark sesame oil

2 tablespoons cornstarch

2 tablespoons cold water

Chopped cilantro or sliced green onions for garnish

SLOW COOKER DIRECTIONS

1. Combine chicken broth, chicken, mushrooms, bamboo shoots, vinegar, soy sauce and chili paste in slow cooker. Cover; cook on LOW 3 to 4 hours.

2. Stir in tofu and sesame oil. Blend cornstarch and water until smooth. Stir into slow cooker. Cover; cook on HIGH 15 minutes or until soup is thickened.

3. Serve hot; garnish with cilantro.

Makes 4 servings

Prep Time: 10 to 15 minutes
Cook Time: 3 to 4 hours (LOW) • 2 to 3 hours (HIGH)

Simmering Hot & Sour Soup

Szechwan Shrimp Stir-Fry

6 ounces uncooked spaghetti or Chinese noodles
¾ pound large raw shrimp, peeled and deveined
¼ cup soy sauce
½ teaspoon red pepper flakes
2 teaspoons dark sesame oil
1 cup snow peas
1 red or yellow bell pepper, cut into thin strips
½ cup shredded carrots
2 teaspoons fresh or bottled minced ginger
1½ teaspoons fresh or bottled minced garlic
3 tablespoons water
2 teaspoons cornstarch
¼ cup thinly sliced green onions or chopped fresh cilantro

1. Cook spaghetti according to package directions. Drain; keep warm.

2. Combine shrimp, soy sauce and red pepper flakes in small bowl; toss to coat. Set aside.

3. Heat oil in large nonstick skillet or wok over medium-high heat. Add snow peas, bell pepper, carrots, ginger and garlic; stir-fry 3 minutes.

4. Remove shrimp from bowl, reserving soy sauce mixture. Add shrimp to skillet; stir-fry 2 minutes.

5. Combine water and cornstarch in small bowl; mix well. Add to skillet with reserved soy sauce mixture; stir-fry 2 minutes or until shrimp are pink and opaque and sauce thickens. Serve over spaghetti; garnish with green onions.

Makes 4 servings

Szechwan Shrimp Stir-Fry

Cantonese Tomato Beef

1 beef flank steak or beef tenderloin tail, trimmed (about 1 pound)
2 tablespoons soy sauce
2 tablespoons Asian sesame oil, divided
1 tablespoon plus 1 teaspoon cornstarch, divided
1 pound Chinese-style thin wheat noodles
1 cup beef broth
2 tablespoons brown sugar
1 tablespoon cider vinegar
2 tablespoons vegetable oil, divided
1 tablespoon minced fresh ginger
3 small onions (about 7 ounces), cut into wedges
2 pounds ripe tomatoes (5 large), cored and cut into wedges
1 green onion with top, diagonally cut into thin slices

1. Cut flank steak lengthwise in half, then crosswise into ¼-inch-thick slices. Combine soy sauce, 1 tablespoon sesame oil and 1 teaspoon cornstarch in large bowl. Add beef strips; toss to coat. Set aside to marinate.

2. Cook noodles according to package directions. Drain; toss with remaining 1 tablespoon sesame oil. Keep warm. Combine beef broth, brown sugar, remaining 1 tablespoon cornstarch and vinegar in small bowl; set aside.

3. Heat wok over high heat 1 minute. Drizzle 1 tablespoon vegetable oil into wok and heat 30 seconds. Add ginger and stir-fry about 30 seconds. Add beef mixture and stir-fry 5 minutes. Remove beef to bowl and set aside.

4. Add remaining 1 tablespoon vegetable oil to wok. Add onion wedges; cook and stir about 2 minutes or until wilted. Stir in ½ of tomato wedges. Stir broth mixture and add to wok. Cook and stir until liquid boils and thickens.

5. Return beef and any juices to wok. Add remaining tomato wedges; cook and stir until heated through. Sprinkle with green onion. Serve with cooked noodles.

Makes 4 servings

Acknowledgments

The publisher would like to thank the companies and organizations listed below for the use of their recipes and photographs in this publication.

California Tree Fruit Agreement

Hormel Foods, Carapelli USA, LLC and Melting Pot Foods Inc.

Jennie-O Turkey Store®

McIlhenny Company (TABASCO® brand Pepper Sauce)

National Fisheries Institute

National Honey Board

Nestlé USA

Reckitt Benckiser Inc.

StarKist Seafood Company

USA Rice Federation

Notes

Metric Chart

VOLUME MEASUREMENTS (dry)

$1/8$ teaspoon = 0.5 mL
$1/4$ teaspoon = 1 mL
$1/2$ teaspoon = 2 mL
$3/4$ teaspoon = 4 mL
1 teaspoon = 5 mL
1 tablespoon = 15 mL
2 tablespoons = 30 mL
$1/4$ cup = 60 mL
$1/3$ cup = 75 mL
$1/2$ cup = 125 mL
$2/3$ cup = 150 mL
$3/4$ cup = 175 mL
1 cup = 250 mL
2 cups = 1 pint = 500 mL
3 cups = 750 mL
4 cups = 1 quart = 1 L

VOLUME MEASUREMENTS (fluid)

1 fluid ounce (2 tablespoons) = 30 mL
4 fluid ounces ($1/2$ cup) = 125 mL
8 fluid ounces (1 cup) = 250 mL
12 fluid ounces ($1 1/2$ cups) = 375 mL
16 fluid ounces (2 cups) = 500 mL

WEIGHTS (mass)

$1/2$ ounce = 15 g
1 ounce = 30 g
3 ounces = 90 g
4 ounces = 120 g
8 ounces = 225 g
10 ounces = 285 g
12 ounces = 360 g
16 ounces = 1 pound = 450 g

DIMENSIONS

$1/16$ inch = 2 mm
$1/8$ inch = 3 mm
$1/4$ inch = 6 mm
$1/2$ inch = 1.5 cm
$3/4$ inch = 2 cm
1 inch = 2.5 cm

OVEN TEMPERATURES

250°F = 120°C
275°F = 140°C
300°F = 150°C
325°F = 160°C
350°F = 180°C
375°F = 190°C
400°F = 200°C
425°F = 220°C
450°F = 230°C

BAKING PAN SIZES

Utensil	Size in Inches/Quarts	Metric Volume	Size in Centimeters
Baking or	8×8×2	2 L	20×20×5
Cake Pan	9×9×2	2.5 L	23×23×5
(square or	12×8×2	3 L	30×20×5
rectangular)	13×9×2	3.5 L	33×23×5
Loaf Pan	8×4×3	1.5 L	20×10×7
	9×5×3	2 L	23×13×7
Round Layer	8×1½	1.2 L	20×4
Cake Pan	9×1½	1.5 L	23×4
Pie Plate	8×1¼	750 mL	20×3
	9×1¼	1 L	23×3
Baking Dish	1 quart	1 L	—
or Casserole	1½ quart	1.5 L	—
	2 quart	2 L	—